SIBLING GROUPS AND SOCIAL WORK

Sibling Groups and Social Work

A study of children referred for permanent substitute family placement

PETER WEDGE
GREG MANTLE

Avebury

Aldershot · Brookfield USA · Hong Kong · Singapore · Sydney

HV
875.58
.G7
W43
1991

© Peter Wedge and Greg Mantle 1991

All rights reserved. No part of this publication may be reproduced, stored in a retrieval system, or transmitted in any form or by any means, electronic, mechanical, photocopying, recording, or otherwise without the prior permission of the publisher.

Published by
Avebury
Academic Publishing Group
Gower House
Croft Road
Aldershot
Hants GU11 3HR

Gower Publishing Company
Old Post Road
Brookfield
Vermont 05036
USA

A CIP catalogue record for this book
is available from the British Library.

ISBN 1 85628 195 7

Printed and Bound in Great Britain by
Athenaeum Press Ltd., Newcastle upon Tyne.

LONGWOOD COLLEGE LIBRARY
FARMVILLE, VIRGINIA 23901

Contents

List of tables	vii
Acknowledgements	ix

1 Introduction — 1
  Current practice and broad issues — 3
  A climate of concern — 4
  The impact of a small sibling group on an existing family — 5

2 Current state of knowledge — 7
  The nature and importance of sibling relationships — 8
  Sibling relationships and social work — 12
  Maintaining links between separated family members — 14
  Factors associated with successful permanent placements — 20
  Indicators of success — 24

3 The study — 26
  The sample — 27

4 The children — 30
  Characteristics of the groups — 31
  Source of referral — 32
  Length of time in care before referral — 33
  Links with the family of origin — 33

Special needs	34
Patterns of sibling-sibling interaction	35

5 Placement practices and placement experiences — 37
First documented aim	37
Reasons for chosen aims	38
Prime movers in setting aims	40
First permanent placements	40
Length of time on referral	41
Type of placement	41
Unplaced children	43
Aims and placements	45
Placement and disruption	45
The new families	46
Second permanent placements	47
Links between separated siblings	47

6 The disruptions — 49
Disruption and age on referral	51
Reasons for disruption	52
The sibling dimension in disruptions	53
Factors associated with disruption	55
Anomalous findings	59
Special needs, step-siblings and disruption	60
New step-siblings	61
Age structure of children in substitute families	61
Disruption and age at referral	63
Previous parenting experience	64
Time in care	65
Age of substitute mother	67
Child's age, special needs and behaviour problems	69
The most important variables	72

7 Overview on work with sibling groups — 73
Numbers of sibling groups	73
Children placed	74
Maintaining or splitting the groups	74
Disruptions	75
Factors associated with disruption	76
Links between family members	78
Implications for social work practice	80
Conclusion	83

References	**85**
Appendix: information gathered for the study	**91**
Index of authors	**94**

List of tables

3.1	Children referred: sibling groups and others	27
4.1	Characteristics of the groups	31
4.2	Age and gender of children referred (in completed years of age)	32
4.3	Source of referral of children by sector	32
4.4	Age by length of time in care (pre-referral)	33
4.5	Recorded 'special needs'	34
4.6	Age by 'special needs' (other than 'sibling group')	35
5.1	Documented aim: maintain, split or splinter by sector (children)	38
5.2	Reasons for chosen aims (documented)	38
5.3	Length of time on referral before first placement	41
5.4	Type of placement by agency sector	42
5.5	Type of placement by length of time on referral	42

5.6	Placed/unplaced by age at referral	43
5.7	Outcome for 'unplaced' children	44
5.8	Type of placement by disruption	46
5.9	New families	46
6.1	Outcomes of referral by sector	50
6.2	Disruption by age on referral	51
6.3	Reasons for disruption	52
6.4	Expectation in disruptions	53
6.5	Association of sibling factors in disruptions	53
6.6	Nature of sibling factor in disruptions	54
6.7	Individual factors associated with disruption	57
6.8	Average number of step-siblings by number of special needs and disruption	60
6.9	Disruption by number of new step-siblings	61
6.10	Study children placed with other children: disruption and age factors	62
6.11	Disruption by age at referral (Groups A, B and C)	63
6.12	Presence of new step-siblings by previous parenting experience	65
6.13	Length of time in care by disruption (Groups A, B and C)	66
6.14	Age of substitute mother by disruption (Groups A, B and C)	67
6.15	Mean age of mothers by disruption and number of special needs in children (Group C)	68
6.16	Additional 'special needs' and age group by disruption (Groups A, B and C)	69
6.17	Age (in complete years) by placement disruption (Groups A, B and C) - Children with a behaviour problem	70
6.18	Children having additional special needs by placement group within age groups (percentaged)	71

Acknowledgements

The investigation reported here would have been impossible without the help and support of a host of people, too numerous to mention individually. They include managers, social work practitioners and clerical staff of the five voluntary agencies; the Director of Social Services for Essex and the staff of the Family Finding Units; all who helped with the piloting, particularly Elisabeth Traverse and Christine Shackell; Sally Banks of the Social Services Inspectorate; Rosalind Niblett of British Agencies for Adoption and Fostering and Sue Wates of the Thomas Coram Adoption Agency prompted the enquiry and sustained interest and encouragement throughout; the grant given by Access Four enabled the project to be carried out and was much appreciated; our colleagues at the University of East Anglia, and particularly June Thoburn, have helped with their wide knowledge in relevant related fields; Steve Mosley and Jacqui White proved invaluable with their data processing expertise; Toby Lewis made an indispensable contribution in elucidating the statistics; our families have put up with the inevitable disruption that research seems to bring to domestic routine; finally Anne Borrett performed wonders in converting our rough hewn drafts into legible and attractive typescript.

To everyone we extend our thanks in the hope that, while the end product is clearly our final responsibility, it is nevertheless work with which they are pleased to have been associated.

Peter Wedge
Greg Mantle

1 Introduction

From time immemorial some children have grown up in a family different from that into which they were born; innumerable pieces of literature bear witness to the pains and the pleasures of the experience; the fate of separated brothers and sisters has often featured in legend and folk-tale. Today, professional child care social workers in Western societies are frequently in a position to consolidate or separate existing groups of brothers and sisters, and to reunite sibling groups already divided or sustain their separation.

Through most of history the placement of a child in an alternative family has been dependent on custom, sanguinity and commercial considerations. In Britain, it is only during the last half century that efforts have been made by professional child care agencies to arrange placement according to scientific principles. In a general sense, the objective has been to secure the best alternative parenting available for children whose biological parents were unable or unwilling to undertake their upbringing.

Of course, the locating of children in a family different from that into which they were born is not only the function of professional child care agencies. When parents separate then the disposition of their children could well be settled by mutual agreement, without the involvement of any third party. In divorce situations or where agreement between the parents cannot be reached, then magistrates, judges, local authority social workers, probation officers and guardians ad litem could also play a part. The increasing numbers of children growing up in reconstituted families bears witness to the extent to which decisions are being made daily by parents and professionals; these decisions have far-reaching consequences for the health, education and development of large numbers of children and constitute a social issue of major and mounting importance.

Of vital importance to decisions about placements in alternative, substitute or reconstituted families has been the consideration of a child's experiences in the family of origin and of the role played by other family members. Studies of child development have revealed the relevance of home and family to physical, emotional and cognitive growth (see, for example, Pringle, 1974), and increasingly research is providing insights into the way that families and substitute families contribute to healthy and/or damaged beings (e.g. Madge, 1983). In placing children for fostering or adoption, courts, social workers and other professionals have increasingly turned to psychological and psychiatric research; additionally, there is a growing body of research which specifically explores placement practice and the outcome of placement decisions for children's developmental health (e.g. Wedge and Thoburn, 1986; Rowe, et al., 1984.)

However, such research is not only incomplete but it is decidedly patchy. Some issues have received a great deal of attention whereas others have been barely identified as important for exploration. As far as family members are concerned, mothers have had most attention, fathers much less, and siblings hardly any.

For at least forty years there has been considerable interest in the mother-child bond and its importance in child development and in pathology. Work summarised by Rutter (1981) was extensive and while questioning some of the early conclusions of Bowlby (1951), the leading and highly influential investigator, it did indicate the emphasis given by research to the crucial nature of this relationship.

More recently, the role played by fathers in child development has increasingly attracted attention and a growing literature reflects this further dimension (e.g. Parke, 1981); Lamb (1982b) has written a short review of research into the relevance for young children's emotional development.

It is only very recently that research has begun to address sibling relationships and their importance (e.g. Lamb and Sutton-Smith (1982); Dunn and Kendrick (1982); Dunn (1984); Dunn (1988b).

In 1984 the Eastern Counties Group of Adoption Agencies invited Arnon Bentovim, a well-known child psychiatrist, to lead them in a workshop to review practice in respect of sibling groups of children. He carried out a search for available literature and research material to provide the group with relevant reading matter. This confirmed an enormous gap in the theoretical knowledge base, with sparse information or research on sibling relationships within natural or birth families, and virtually nothing on sibling placement in substitute families. (For an account of issues raised at the workshop see Jones and Niblett, (1985)).

Current practice and broad issues

Despite this lack of knowledge, social work with families which include siblings is routine; moreover, the placement of siblings is the routine business of fostering and adoption workers in two ways. First, sibling groups of children are received into local authority care and require placement. One issue is whether in the circumstances it is better for all the brothers and/or sisters to be placed together or for the group to be split so that various individuals or sub-groups are in different foster or adoptive families. This is the main issue which prompted the enquiry covered in this account. It raises questions about present practice and the beliefs and knowledge which underlie it. In what situations and for which children is placement with siblings likely to prove essential, or preferable, or at the other extreme disastrous? For example, if siblings love each other or hate each other is either circumstance a reason for maintaining or for splitting a group? In what ways do siblings matter to each other, and which of these ways is important in the context of placement with a permanent substitute family? What factors in sibling relationships, then, are pointers to the need to keep the group entirely together, or to separate them? What priority should be given to preserving or disrupting sibling groups when deciding on the 'least detrimental alternative placement'? If groups are separated, what factors should influence judgements about enabling contact between siblings?

The second way in which social workers are involved routinely in the placement of siblings is much more pervasive. By far the majority of children in the total population - in excess of 80 per cent - belong to sibling groups; predictably, a majority of children coming into care will also be members of families where there are brothers and sisters, half-brothers or half-sisters, step-brothers or step-sisters. In many instances, however, not all of the children will be received into care and often there will be only one individual child. In effect, sibling groups are often being split up at the point of entry into public care.

Again, this raises issues about the precise nature of present practice and the beliefs and knowledge underlying it. Similar questions arise over admission to care as over placement of groups already in care. They focus on conflict between individual, sub-group and total group 'treatment' for sibling children; further, if siblings are not to remain as a total group, then the nature, extent and means of 'access' to one another becomes the next consideration.

Given the paucity of information generally about the number of sibling groups for whom the child care system needs to make provision, and the grounds for maintaining or separating siblings, it seemed best in the work reported here to concentrate in the first instance on some specific questions and to narrow the focus of research in an attempt to achieve a modest initial fact-finding aim to inform both practice and further research as necessary. Because of the expressed interest of members of the Eastern Counties Group of Adoption Agencies, the research itself addressed specifically the outcome for those sibling groups referred to adoption agencies for permanent substitute placement.

The central issue which prompted the investigation was whether and in what circumstances it appeared better to separate groups of siblings when placing them for adoption (or long-term fostering). In order to begin to answer such a question, however, it was necessary to define what is meant by 'better', and to design an appropriate piece of research which could take account of the key factors that influence placement outcome, but could also reflect the volume of sibling groups for whom placement is required. This last point is of crucial importance since there is almost no published information about the extent to which sibling groups are split at placement; this was vital if a study were to be founded on a large enough number of cases to justify some general statements, however tentative. In a broad sense, the research was concerned to establish what was taking place in the matter of sibling placement and what lessons might be learnt about policies and practices.

A climate of concern

Dispassionate examination of the facts about the permanent placement of sibling groups is bedevilled in two important ways. First, even suggesting that kin might be better separated seems inevitably to arouse strong emotional responses (e.g. Ward, 1984; Cowley, 1987). Secondly, as already mentioned, very few facts have been available for consideration, beyond the 'case specific'.

Recent examples of the case-study approach have been provided by Nix (1983), Dresser (1985), and by Morrison and Brown (1986). Although the material presented by such examples is of inherent interest to all concerned in this field, it is not particularly useful as an aid to future decision-making. Policy-makers and practitioners require a more general guide than can be supplied by individual case studies. The temptation to draw pointers for future practice from too little evidence has to be avoided. One author (Forbes, 1977) presents five apparently universal criteria for the separation of siblings on the basis of fifteen clinical cases.

There have been exceptions to this small-scale approach. Notably, Aldridge and Cautley (1976) studied 115 foster home placements; also, a number of major research projects have explored the sibling dimension briefly, en passant, as for example Fanshel and Shinn (1978), Rowe et al. (1984), and Millham et al. (1986). Both Cutler (1984) and Berridge and Cleaver (1987) specifically addressed 'siblings' in foster care placements, but the sibling dimension in permanency work has to date received very little attention. The recent study by Thoburn and Rowe (1988) adds to our knowledge specifically about the permanent placement of children with special needs, including some information about sibling groups maintained intact on placement.

The recognition of a knowledge gap is not new. Timberlake and Hamlin (1982), and Clifton (1985) have pointed to it; most vividly Jones and Niblett (op. cit.) warned that 'to continue to make decisions about separating or maintaining sibling groups within the poverty of our current knowledge and assessment skills may pose unacceptable risks. It may be the unacceptable face of family placement in the late 1980s.' Cousins (1989) addressing short-term fostering urged that special family units be established to ensure that sibling groups could be kept together in residential but 'quasi-domestic' settings rather than split them between foster homes.

The impact of a small sibling group on an existing family

As adults we tend to spend our time in groups of various sizes alternated with brief periods of time alone. The relative proportions will, of course, vary from individual to individual according to personal circumstances and preferences. Probably the most intense group experience for most people is that of their nuclear family either as children or as parents themselves. Undoubtedly, one of the particular stresses with which parents have to deal when handling a family of children is the demands made upon them and the interactions with which they have to cope, both those between their children and themselves and those that occur between children but which need to be 'monitored'.

It is striking how the number of possible interactions escalates with the introduction of siblings into a new family. For example, as Figure 1 shows, an original group of two parents and a child might have three possible two-way interactions and one three-way interaction.

Figure 1.1
Impact on number of interactions:
adding <u>two</u> siblings to groups of various sizes

<u>Original group</u>: ABC -> AB, AC, BC + ABC

<u>New group</u>: ABC with DE -> AB, AC, BC
AD, BD, CD,
AE, BE, CE,
DE.

+ ABC, ABD, ABE.
BCD, BCE, ACD,
ACE. ADE. BDE.
CDE.

<u>Original group</u>: AB -> AB

<u>New group</u>: AB with CD -> AB, AC, AD,
BC. BD. CD.

+ ABC. ABD. ACD. BCD.

However, if this group of two adults (A and B) and a child (C) is joined by two siblings (D and E) on placement, then the number of possible two-way interactions increases from three to ten; moreover, the number of possible three-way interactions (including those involving the parents) increases from one to ten.

Figure 1.1 also shows the impact of two siblings (C and D) on a childless couple (A and B). There the number of possible two-way interactions increases from one to six, and the three-way interactions from nought to four.

Of course, with the introduction of even larger groups of siblings these changes become even more pronounced. There is no need, however, to dwell on the point further, it is obvious that simply in terms of the potential interactions, the impact of siblings upon a pre-existing family is considerable if not dramatic.

2 Current state of knowledge

The aspect of social work practice which most sharply points up the actual or potential importance of siblings to each other is probably the decision about placement in a permanent substitute family. In deciding on the placement of a sibling group several crucial issues arise. First among these is the nature of the relationships between the siblings concerned and the relevance of them to the decision about whether or not to split the siblings at the time of placement. It is important, therefore, to understand the contribution that sibling relationships make to child development, an area which is informed by relatively limited research. Secondly, it is possible that particular aspects of sibling relationships are important in reaching social work decisions about individual children, and that these specific aspects are different for disturbed or deprived children than for those growing up in more normal situations. In any event, decisions about maintaining sibling groups or splitting them will need to take into account the links that it might be possible to maintain between separated family members after the placement has occurred. This is a third issue which needs to be explored in developing our enquiry.

Apart from questions of sibling relationships and family links, then a successful permanent placement will depend on a range of other factors which are independent of the sibling dimension, although the sibling dimension is clearly an element in placement outcome. Rushton et al. (1989) pointed out the difficulties presented for substitute families by sibling groups. In addition to the 'normal' dynamics encountered in biological families there is the impact of changing caretakers, changing environments and, often, changing groupings of siblings. Further, a range of criteria can be employed in defining placement 'success', a measure which is essential if any assessment is to be made about the appropriateness of splitting or maintaining sibling groups. The most frequently used indicator is that of placement disruption, though this phenomenon itself is open to a variety of interpretations (see Rowe, 1987).

In this chapter these various strands will be explored in order to establish the extent to which existing literature can inform both social work practice and research into sibling placement.

The nature and importance of sibling relationships

'Sibling influences begin even before the second child is born, for the anticipation of the youngster's birth affects the parents as well as their relationships with and availability to their first-born offspring,' (Lamb, 1982(a)). But if the relevance of a sibling begins to be felt before birth, in most normal situations siblings continue to be relevant throughout childhood and adulthood. Dunn (1984) noted that while the extent of sibling influences on the development of adult personality was as yet imprecisely known, 'we can say that the power of the relationship lasts far beyond childhood; it withstands the separation of time and space, and provides important emotional security for most people in the later stages of their lives.'

Dunn observes that sibling relationships often last a lifetime and are of real importance to the majority of individuals even in their old age. Indeed, not infrequently siblings resume life in a shared household following the death of marriage partners, thus replicating in their final years something of the close physical relationship with which they will have spent part of their childhood. Undoubtedly, the increasing awareness of siblings' relationships is beginning to prompt more research. For the purpose of this study it is disappointing that more has not yet been carried out.

Among published research, however, Ross and Milgram (1982) argue that the sibling bond has a special quality and pose the question of whether it is psychologically possible ever to dissociate oneself from siblings in the way that old friends or even former marriage partners can be forgotten. Their studies of adult relationships suggest that few siblings ever consider the breaking of ties, even in situations involving severe hostility. Other writers, however, appear to accord no such special status to sibling relationships. Youniss (1980), for example, holds that two specific relations constitute the basic make-up of society as experienced by children, namely those with adults and those with peers. Thus, sibling relationships are treated as if they were a sub-set of peer relationships.

Where sibling relationships have been held to justify investigation in their own right, differences in the nature and quality of the relationships have tended to be explained in terms of birth order, gender, age-gap or family size.

Much weight has been accorded to each of these factors although supportive empirical evidence has not always been provided. Wilson and Edington (1982), for example, in their study of birth order effects among pairs of siblings, link birth order causally with the quality of relationships and with longer term consequences for the individuals concerned. 'In the two-sibling family it [birth order] can always be relied on to point out the origins of significant life-long attitudes and to deepen and enrich our knowledge of what makes us tick.'

The limitations of such an approach, in which life circumstances of this kind tend to have been examined in isolation, has been criticised by Dunn (1984) who notes that while autobiographical accounts have often stressed the importance of siblings, psychologists tend to date to have focussed 'not on the impact of different kinds of sibling relationships - affectionate, conflict-ridden, jealous, domineering - instead, they have made numerous attempts to establish how far birth-order, sex of sibling, and the age-gap between siblings affect children.'

Dunn's view is that to explain the ways in which brothers and sisters influence one another it must first be recognized that a complicated equation is involved, taking into account 'not only age and sex, but the personalities of the children, the size of the family, the social circumstances, and most importantly the children's relations with their parents.' Because so many varied factors affect relationships between siblings, simple clear connections should not be expected between a child's position in the family or the sex of his sibling on the one hand, and the way the children get along or how their personalities develop on the other.

When it comes to the ways in which siblings influence one another's development though, Dunn (1984) points out that 'the sex and personality of the firstborn is more likely to influence the later born children in a direct way than vice versa ... Firstborn are more likely to express ambivalence or hostility than later born.' Dunn stresses, however, that birth-order, age-gap or gender are not necessarily or simply related to the extent of intimacy and affection that a child feels and shows towards a sibling, and that it is this which is probably of prime importance in influencing the sibling.

This emphasis on the limited value of 'sibling status' in explaining development has also been remarked upon by Lamb (1982a) in commenting on new directions in sibling research. Among the changes is the switch from the identification of sibling status effects to an exploration of the processes whereby effects are mediated; the other changes include the recognition that cross-species and cross-cultural research can be informative (see Weisner, 1982), and the emergence of a 'life-span developmental psychology' which proposes that development is continuous, a view which demands a shift in research from emphasising only the long-term consequences of early experiences (see also Clarke and Clarke, 1976).

One value of cross-cultural studies is that they help us to question our own preconceptions about the nature of siblingship itself. Western societies define this in terms of blood-ties, but it might not be this which makes sibling relationships 'special'. Perhaps it is the length and intensity of shared experience. In due course, studies of fostered and adopted children can help to inform this issue.

Undoubtedly the aspect of sibling interaction which has received most attention in the literature is 'sibling rivalry'. Its negative effects have long been discussed (for example, see Levy, 1934 and 1937). Such rivalry can lead to quite powerful conflict which has been found to vary according to differences of gender, family position, etc.. Sutton-Smith and Rosenberg (1970) reported that boys were more likely to employ 'attack and offence' while girls used reasoning, defence and making their sibling feel obligated. First-born children were more likely to boss, attack, interfere, ignore (paradoxically!), be offensive or bribe their sibling; second-born children tended to attack property, plead or reason with siblings. Koch (1960) found that a pair of brothers seemed to produce more quarrelling than any other combination of siblings. Bank and Kahn (1982a), however, found more positive aspects in childhood fighting. 'Aggressiveness is a major vehicle for sibling interaction and, as such, has had a broad utility for human beings. Aggression, even when painful, represents contact, warmth, another presence.'

Other dimensions of sibling interaction which have prompted research interest include: 'loyalty' (Bank and Kahn, 1982b); 'caretaking' both where siblings teach siblings (Cicirelli, 1976 and Stewart, 1984) and where the care-taking is therapeutic (Greenbaum, 1965; Lavigueur, 1976 both cited by Bryant 1982); the distinctive nature of roles adopted in pretend play between pre-school siblings (Dale, 1989); and responses to a handicapped sibling (Brody and Stoneman, 1982; and Meyer et al., 1986). Attention has also been paid to the roles taken by siblings in and outside the home. Sutton-Smith (1966) found that in play, first-born children took high-power roles with siblings and low-power roles with non-sibling friends; later-born children took low-power roles with older siblings but high-power roles with friends. This suggests that the younger siblings modelled their play behaviour on older siblings, acting as if they were an older sibling in power interactions rather than reiterating their 'younger-sibling' behaviour patterns. This is a potentially important finding which could help in understanding children's responses to changes in their social environment.

Boer (1990) in a Dutch study of siblings aged 6 yrs. to 12 yrs. in intact two-child families found that the children gave a 'very positive impression of their relationship with their brother or sister'; for this age group 'warmth' and 'conflict' appeared to co-exist in sibling inter-actions. Again, there was a pattern of second-born children showing 'more prosocial behaviour' towards their siblings than they perceive from them. In addition to family factors, there are indications that temperament (or 'behavioural style') is of particular relevance.

In a review of sibling influences on childhood development, Dunn (1988a) identified six main points:

1. Children's style of conflict behaviour and their 'co-operative fantasy play', as well as their development of aggressive behaviour, seems likely to be causally influenced by siblings.

2. Other than for aggressive behaviour, there appears not to be a causal link with problems in the sibling relationship, although such problems can be indicative of other problems.

3. Because the quality of sibling relationships is strongly influenced by family factors, the two elements should be considered together. Thus in examining 'sibling influence' account should be taken of 'differential parental behaviour and the emotional climate of the family.'

4. The heightened importance of these family factors is found by studies of families under stress.

5. There is suggestive evidence, as yet not conclusive, that 'later born siblings are influenced by first born in socio-cognitive development and gender identity.'

6. Research is increasingly and importantly addressing the issue of 'why siblings develop to be so different from one another.'

Her own detailed research (Dunn 1988b) showed how children from as early as 18 months of age onwards have some notion of how to influence the feelings of a sibling, and to know just what particular objects or activities are especially significant for the sibling. The interactions which were studied revealed 'the beginnings of an understanding of certain rules of positive justice' and indicated in the young children a practical awareness of 'how such rules can be used when one's interests are threatened.' Indeed, Dunn concluded that 'children are motivated to understand the social rules and relationships of their cultural world because they need to get things done in their family relationships.' Inter-sibling exchanges are among the important means by which children learn to function as social beings.

Nothing in this overview undermines the importance of the study of sibling relationships or of knowledge of sibling relationships when placing children in permanent substitute families. The nature of the importance and the interpretation of specific relationships is still fraught with difficulty, however. If sibling relationships themselves are dependent upon other family relationships, then what does this mean for situations in which children are quite deliberately placed in a new family?

Sibling relationships and social work

As has been argued, sibling relationships are an important consideration in adoption and fostering work, in divorce, custody and access decisions, and in the use of local authority social work for children and families generally. In all of these areas of social work the maintenance of family links for children is a major consideration.

Millham et al. (1986) reported that of their study population of 450 children in care, only 11 per cent had no half-, step- or natural siblings. They also indicated that although formal access restrictions were generally applied only to parental contact, siblings were neither sought out nor encouraged to visit by social workers. Nearly half of the children under study entered care with one or more siblings, a factor which was seen as a considerable restriction to placement options.

Rowe et al. (1984) in their study of 145 foster children, found that 84 per cent were known to have full- or half-siblings. In 57 per cent of these cases at least one sibling was known to be in care or to have been adopted, and in the other cases all the child's siblings were at home with one or both parents. Twenty-five per cent had at least one sibling in the same foster home. At the time of the research, 10 per cent of the study children were in contact with one or more siblings in other foster homes or residential placements, but meetings tended to be infrequent. Moreover, where a study child had a sibling in care, there was frequently no contact, even where there was a lack of contact with any other family member.

Wedge and Phelan (1986) studied children in the care of a local authority over a four-year period and found that less than one-in-five was an only child; a third of the children had been admitted to care at the same time as a sibling.

Clearly, all the evidence shows that the majority of children entering care have siblings; the maintenance of appropriate links itself appears to be a neglected social work dimension. The growing isolation of children and adolescents from their families of origin through care careers as reported for example by Millham et al. (1986) and Packman et al. (1986) would strongly suggest that the 'links-perspective' needs far greater attention from policy-makers and practitioners than it has been receiving. It is a perspective which brings into sharp focus issues of joint or single placement, of access, and of 'grief' work with all siblings taken into care and with those who remain in the natural family.

Turning specifically to adoption and fostering, Jones and Niblett (1985) posed the question 'to split or not to split' in the placement of siblings and identified a range of potential advantages and disadvantages of maintaining sibling groups. Essentially, the decision for or against joint placement was seen as a weighing of the benefits of family unity and togetherness on the one hand, against the need for stability, security and individual parenting which damaged and disturbed children might require. In their paper, the authors refer to Bentovim's contribution to their deliberations in which he raised three important issues for decision-makers. Two of these serve to highlight the limits to the present state of knowledge. First, it is suggested that learned roles are likely to be carried forward into a new family. While this must to an extent be true, the problem is in deciding which roles these would be. As indicated above, research by Sutton-Smith has shown how children can take on very different roles with peers compared with those which they assume with their siblings. Also, Dunn (1988) has warned of the way in which sibling relationships are themselves dependent on interaction with parents. It might therefore be difficult to predict the role which might be assumed in any new family.

Secondly, Bentovim suggested that if roles and patterns of interaction were assessed to be functional, rather than a combination of dysfunctional and permanently set, this would indicate that siblings should be placed together in a new family. The difficulty here is to know how the 'assessment' might be achieved. Bellwood (1985) cites the urgent need to develop 'a method for evaluating sibling relationships within an overall systematic approach'. In any event, 'functional' has two very different meanings in this context. It can refer to factors which promote the normal development of the child or it can refer to the maintenance of a steady state within the family 'system'. Maintaining family equilibrium may not always serve the child's development since it can be detrimental. Finally, 'permanently set' prompts the question as to whether any role or pattern of interaction can be permanent. (See, again, Clarke and Clarke, 1976).

The upshot of these comments is that the process of assessment, using any of the suggested criteria, continues to be very difficult. Despite this, it has to proceed, with decisions being taken in the absence of clear information and knowledge. In practice, social workers will undoubtedly continue to need to consider the likelihood of maladaptive behaviour appearing, persisting or ceasing in each one of a range of different social environments. The decision, of course, can be informed by the issues identified by Bentovim, as well as by lessons learned from helping foster families through disruption (see Aldgate and Hawley, 1986) and perhaps by the application of attachment theory to sibling relationships (for example, Fahlberg, 1981).

Although 'to split or not to split' is a central issue in the placement of sibling groups, there are a number of others. For example, Bentovim's third issue presses the view that if siblings are split, then practitioners need to assume responsibility for the 'grief work' involved. Further, if a group is split how should the question of access between siblings be addressed? Triseliotis (1985) and Ward (1986) have argued for adoption with access in particular cases. However, most attention has been directed to the continuation of parental rather than sibling contact in such 'open adoptions'. The debate over parental contact is itself far from settled and arguments are tendered for the cessation of contact between child and birth relatives on the grounds that the growth of new attachments may be hindered (Goldstein et al., 1980). On the other hand there are arguments for the continuation of contact to promote the child's identity and offer the agency a 'fall-back' plan if substitute placements cannot be continued (Fratter, 1989). Finally, it should be noted that there is no specific clause in British legislation on child care, adoption, and fostering which prohibits sibling access; on the contrary, while until 1989 there was nothing which specifically encouraged it, the Children Act of that year requires that an authority providing accommodation for siblings should place them together 'so far as is reasonably practical and consistent with [the children's] welfare' (Section 23.7.b).

To summarize, there are clear indications in the extremely thin literature concerning sibling placement in substitute families that very much more needs to be known about the grounds for particular decisions and the consequences of those decisions once made. These decisions concern both the placement of siblings and the maintenance of links between them.

Maintaining links between separated family members

The terms 'access', 'contact', 'visits', 'links' are frequently employed as if they were readily interchangeable. Such a lack of consistency in precision allows, for example, the sending of birthday cards to be described in the same terms as a weekly 'stay-over'. In what follows, 'links' will used as an umbrella word to include both 'access' and 'contact'. By 'access' is implied face-to-face meetings occurring other than by chance and either formally organized by an external party (e.g. a social worker) or informally agreed by family members. 'Contact' includes telephone conversations, written communication and all other liaison excluding face-to-face meeting. These definitions follow the Code of Practice on Access (DHSS, 1983).

There are major differences in the attitudes and practices of professionals in dealing with children separated from other family members according to whether the practice concerns children in care, adoption, or children of divorce. These attitudes and practices reflect both the law and the attitude of society as a whole. They will be considered separately.

Children in care

The growing literature stemming from research into children in care confirms the importance of maintaining links between the child and the family of origin. For example, Millham et al. (1986) suggested that 'aspects of the care situation, particularly the difficulty of providing stable substitute parenting, makes home and family contact very important to the child. This is reinforced by the fact that a child's withering relationships with the family makes an early exit from care unlikely.'

Morris (1984) cited the wealth of British and American research evidence supporting the need for children in care to retain close links with their parents, and with the one notable exception of Goldstein et al. (1973) who drew on clinical experience, there appears to be a consensus that links should be maintained. There is even some direct consumer evidence to this effect from children themselves (Page and Clark, 1977).

Nevertheless, despite the recognition that maintaining links brings potential advantage, the growing isolation of children from their birth families as they advance through care careers has been well documented. (In addition to Millham et al. 1986, see Fanshel and Shinn, 1978, Holman, 1980, Rowe et al., 1984, and Packman, 1986). Accounting for this paradoxical state of affairs is not easy. Millham et al. (1986) found, for example, that two-fifths of all long-stay children in care had no parental contacts after two years, yet in two-thirds of these cases there was no social work reason for this exclusion. Links with the wider family were also found to be tenuous.

For children in residential care there would appear to be least justification for severing links. Indeed, Maier (1981) has called for the child, parents and care-workers to become full 'partners' in residential group care, to become 'co-caregivers' who are 'actually co-parenting'.

In foster-care, Holman (1980) suggested that most foster parents operate on an exclusive model of fostering, encouraging the severing of ties with birth families. Rowe et al. (1984) reported that children in long-term foster care feared a conflict of loyalties and did not want to upset their foster parents. Views about the desirable frequency of access quite often differed between natural parents, children, social workers and foster parents so that 'the views of all participants form a tangled web with ambivalence and support for the status quo much in evidence.' Rowe's research suggests that the social worker may face conflicting demands from the various participants involved in the care situation and therefore the early encouragement of access is most likely to ensure its continuation in the longer-term. The importance of the worker's role in facilitating this was emphasised by Fanshel and Shinn (1978), by Aldgate (1980) and more recently by Johnson (1986). Also, Proch and Howard (1986) in their study of foster children in Illinois found that most parents who were scheduled to visit did indeed do so in compliance with the schedule specified in the caseplan; in contrast, there was little visiting by parents who did not have a schedule or who were told to request a visit when they wanted one. The need for access to be well-defined has been documented by Donley (1978) and by Aldgate and Hawley (1986) in their studies of disruptions in foster placements. In total, the evidence suggests that if links are seen to be desirable then the best way of maintaining them is for the worker quickly to establish a well-defined pattern which all parties seem likely to accept as time proceeds.

The precise nature of such links, though, remains problematic. Barber (1985) argued that they must be seen in the context of the overall plan for the child. Where shared care or rehabilitation is the social work objective, then the maintenance of links is not significantly at issue. Permanent separations, on the other hand, are more problematic in terms of whether or not to maintain links and, if so, in what form and with what frequency. Although Barber listed eight 'key points' to consider in assessing the need for links, there appears to be no suggestion by the author of how these points might be weighed in order to reach decisions. The key factor seems to be the extent to which maintaining links can contribute to the child's need for attachment, security and identity.

From the perspective of the study reported here the particularly striking feature of the literature about links is its focus upon the parental dimension to the exclusion of members of the wider family. There are signs that this is beginning to change. For example, Rowe et al. (1984) unreservedly commended the continuation of links between their study children and birth grandparents though they found that children's attitudes to contact with siblings tended to be lukewarm. Although Millham et al. (1986) found that siblings were neither sought out nor encouraged to visit by social workers, it might be argued that sibling links could prove a vital factor in diminishing a child's risk of isolation, particularly where siblings remain at home or a sibling is in a different care placement. In support of this view, Berridge and Cleaver (1987) in their study of long-term fostering found a 'much higher failure rate - 50 per cent - when children are completely separated from their siblings than when they are accompanied by brothers or sisters' in their placements.

Adoption

Successful 'adoption with access' can only occur where there is co-operation between birth and adoptive parents. Although the power exists to attach access conditions to an adoption order (Section 8(7) of the Children Act 1975) courts have been reluctant to use it, preferring either to leave informal arrangements to adopters or not to make the adoption order at all (see Adcock and White, 1985). Fratter (1989) showed that this situation is changing and that agencies can not only place children successfully in adoptive families having contact with birth parents, but that the birth parents can appropriately be involved at times in selecting an adoptive family for their child. In discussing two case examples of 'open adoptions' Ward (1986) argued that the advantages of adoption over long-term fostering are such as strongly to suggest an enhanced use of adoption with access. Thoburn et al. (1986) for their part pointed out that the loss of parental links may be inappropriate especially for older children and urged efforts to achieve 'inclusive permanence' through adoption, custodianship and long-term fostering. Further, from a large-scale survey of 1,165 children with special needs placed with permanent substitute families Fratter et al. (forthcoming) concluded that, allowing for age at placement, children having continued contact with birth parents were no more likely to experience breakdown than those having no contact. Importantly, there was less likelihood of breakdown among older children remaining in touch with siblings who did not share their placement than amongst either those having no contact with any member of the birth family or those in contact with parents.

The significance of such contact for the parties involved should not be under-estimated. In addition to media stories about adult adoptees seeking birth parents, there is research into steps taken by birth parents to locate their children long since given up for adoption (Sawbridge, 1988; Howe, 1988); they bear witness to both the pain and the resolve that separated children and birth parents experience.

The evidence suggests that in matters of adoption the position is even more extreme than with children in care generally. Perhaps a much needed conceptual leap is required generally on the part of practitioners, policy-makers, researchers, parents and children alike, to accept adoption with access (Triseliotis, 1986) and even more especially to maintain links with siblings.

Children of divorce

Where divorce is concerned, maintaining links seems to be taken for granted. Moreover, the number of children involved reaches a quite different scale. In 1984, 144,000 married couples were divorced, 58 per cent of them having children under the age of sixteen; in total some 148,600 children were involved (OPCS, 1986). Over the past twenty years there has been a four-fold increase in the number of divorce decrees absolute in England and Wales (Mitchell, 1985), and Haskey (1982) predicted that one couple in three may now be expected to divorce by their thirtieth wedding anniversary. One child in five in Britain is now likely to experience parental divorce before reaching the age of sixteen, and one in eight before the age of ten years (Haskey, 1983, and Rimmer, 1981).

Of course, the number of divorces does not serve as a reliable indicator of the prevalence of marriage breakdown since many separations occur, both judicial and non-judicial, which may not result in an eventual legal divorce. Additionally, separation of children from parents (and of children from siblings) occurs among the growing number of families where parents are unmarried; no figures are available for such separations.

Given the number of children involved, the maintenance of links is evidently of major importance in this field. Issues concerning the access which the non-custodial parent has with the child are governed by the same 'welfare of the child' principle as that which governs custody (Matrimonial Causes Act, 1973, Section 52), and the courts have an unlimited discretion to make access orders for a child's welfare. Such orders are often routinely made for 'reasonable' access, the details of which are agreed by the divorced parties themselves; alternatively, orders can include specifications about times, days of the week, frequency, and 'staying-over'. In some proceedings grandparents have a statutory right to apply for access.

The weight of current opinion is that maintaining links between child and non-custodial parent assists a child's continuing sense of stability and security. For example, Wallerstein and Kelly (1980) argued that access protects the child against both 'the pain of loss and the psychological impact of that loss'. Also, Murch (1980) noted the child's desire for the absent parent, and Maidment (1984) concluded that if contact with both parents is maintained children cope better with divorce. Given the received benefits of maintaining links, it is a matter of concern that so many are quickly broken. Mitchell (1985) found clear evidence that very soon after separation many children (at least 25 per cent to 30 per cent) lose touch with one parent. Mitchell also found, as did Wallerstein and Kelly, that the pattern of access immediately after separation clearly set the pattern for the future. The sooner and the more frequently that children had access, the more likely were they to keep in touch with the absent parent. Those who had no access in the beginning found problems first in restoring broken relationships and then in maintaining them.

Conciliation services could play an important role in facilitating the maintenance of links. It is significant that in Murch's 1980 study access had ceased shortly after divorce in only 8 per cent of study families who had been visited by divorce court welfare officers, but in 30 per cent of other families.

Very little attention has been given in the divorce literature to the sibling dimension. There is evidence also that it is rarely considered even in welfare reports. Seale (1984), for example, in an examination of half of the Scottish divorce actions involving reports during 1980 identified many gaps in the information made available to the court; the attitude of one or other parent to custody or access was often not mentioned, nor were the children's social relationships with their siblings or other members of the household. Furthermore, Mitchell (1985) found that there was no welfare report at all in most of the cases studied where the children had been divided between the parents.

Approaching the issue of links between siblings who have been separated by the divorce of their parents is handicapped, as other enquiries have been, by the paucity of research on the subject and, in this case, by the general inadequacy of statistical information on the children of divorce. However, Mitchell in her study found that at some stage before divorce, siblings under the age of sixteen had been divided between two parents in 11 per cent of the families studied. This is a higher proportion than that discovered by Eekelaar and Clive (1977) (4 per cent), Murch (1980) (6 per cent) and Maidment (1976) (6 per cent). Mitchell also found that after divorce a further 6 per cent of study families contained siblings who were divided, the interval from divorce to obtaining information being between five and six years.

Applying Mitchell's percentages to figures for England and Wales in 1984 provides an indication of the possible scale of the division of siblings. Among the 48,308 couples who underwent divorce and had more than one child under the age of sixteen, somewhere between 10 and 20 per cent will have involved a division of siblings. This would suggest that the number of children involved would be somewhere in the range of 11,000 to 23,000. This approximation suggests an appreciable number of children, about whom very little is known. Why they are split and how their relationships are affected by the division are two immediate questions to which there are few answers in the literature. Perhaps with the increasing role of divorce court welfare officers this is a situation which will come to be remedied although current indications are that such civil work by the Probation Service is accorded a low priority. (See, for example, the Home Office Statement of National Objectives and Priorities for the Probation Service, Home Office (1984)). Meanwhile, there were three reasons for splitting identified by Mitchell: a request from a child to live with a different parent from the other siblings; children divided by the wish of a parent with little regard to the welfare of the children; and children divided as a way of sharing the burden of care.

The 'splitting' phenomenon reflects the change in attitudes towards fathers having care of children. If only the mothers are expected and expect to perform child-care functions, then it is likely that they will be awarded custody of all children when marriage breaks down. However, as it becomes more commonplace for fathers to perform child-care functions and hence also to gain custody, then the issue of division will more often have to be addressed. Also, the maintenance of links between siblings will have to be considered. For convenience parents could very well attempt to combine their own access with that of siblings. There is, however, some evidence to suggest that this is not likely to be most fruitful. Wallerstein and Kelly (1980) found that where children visit their absent parents jointly with siblings, they are more likely to find the access frustrating than if visiting alone. Combining access could thus carry hazards for both sets of relationships.

Conclusion

Undoubtedly the issue of maintaining links is now receiving attention in child care practice and in child care literature although the emphasis remains essentially on parent-child access and contact (usually mother and child). In the adoption field, the links issue has relatively recently begun to be examined and in the divorce literature the issue has been framed essentially in terms of father-child access. There are clear indications that in all three areas the wider family should be considered and the increasing attention and status given to the role of grandparents is a recognition of this need. The sibling dimension, however, remains almost wholly uncharted.

Factors associated with successful permanent placements

Many authors over the years have played a part in the identification of factors which are likely to contribute towards the success of a placement. Pringle (1967) reviewed adoption research from 1948 to 1965; Jacka (1973) took this research review forward from 1966 to 1972; Rowe et al. (1984) considered long-term foster care; Thoburn et al. (1986) reported on permanence in child care; and Wedge and Thoburn (1986) presented research findings on placing children with special needs. Factors identified in previous work can be grouped as follows:

characteristics of the substitute family;
characteristics of the family of origin;
child variables;
child-care practice variables.

Although this is a useful conceptualisation of relevant factors, it clearly carries limitations in that interactions will undoubtedly occur in many situations. For example, the actions of the social worker in preparing the substitute family may influence their expectations which in turn could determine how successful they feel a placement proves to be.
The objective of a permanent family placement must be 'to provide stability, security and a sense of belonging for children at the hands of adults who genuinely care for them as individuals and with whom, barring unforeseen accidents, they will remain until they are adults or even longer' (Thoburn et al., 1986).

Characteristics of the substitute family

It is a feature of developments in adoption from practice and research that views about necessary characteristics of suitable substitute families have changed. Hapgood (1984) in discussing the selection of adoptive families cites the need for practitioners to take account of demographic variables which may be linked to successful outcome, such as social class, ages of applicants, current family circumstances, marital status and history, geographical mobility, etc.. The author continues, however, by pointing out the absence of studies offering controlled evaluation of variables of this type. In any event, the application of findings from early studies of adoption and fostering to current issues of policy and practice may well be of limited value because of the significant changes which have occurred in the characteristics of the children involved. For example, the early work of Skeels and Harms (1948) linked the intellectual qualities of the adoptive parents with the child's cognitive development in their study of children placed in their adoptive homes when under the age of two. Statistics on adoption now show a continued trend towards older ages at adoption and hence the significance of earlier work to current realities must be questioned.

In a broad sense, however, there is a consensus among early and more recent writers. For example, Pringle (1967) stressed the paramount importance to eventual outcome in adoption of the personal qualities and attitudes of the adopting parents. Similarly, Thoburn et al. (1986) in their study of children with special needs placed in permanent substitute families reach conclusions which reflect the wide range of families with which children can be successfully placed. They found that successful families included some with and some without children of their own; there were some who had previously fostered or adopted and some who had not; there were members of all social classes; also there were 'those whose lives had been happy and uneventful, and those who had had to cope with ill-health, stress and unhappiness in their own lives; those who were principally motivated by self-interest and those whose motivation was mainly altruistic.' In the face of such opposed factors the authors continue by suggesting some characteristics 'often found amongst successful families'. Among others these included 'really enjoying being with children; having some experience of children with special needs; being family-centred and having a strong marriage; believing in self-reliance; being tolerant of others but firmly holding fairly conventional views about how their own lives should be lived.' The authors also found, though, that some successful families 'differed markedly from the majority in all these respects.' The implication here, again, is that when studying substitute parents who have successfully cared for children with special needs, no clear prescription emerges of the ideal family, with characteristics which are universally to be found. The single exception to this is that one characteristic shared by all families appeared to be a 'persistence which at times bordered on stubbornness'. This was also found by Wolkind and Kozaruk (1986) in their study of the placement of children with medical and developmental problems. Families are described as 'far more active than the norm, with a great deal of energy available for community activities and shared family interests. There was often a desire to battle for a child and a definite if slightly affectionate hostility towards professionals, coupled with a wish to prove that they could succeed.'

Characteristics of the natural family

There will be relatively few characteristics of a child's birth family which will directly influence the outcome of a permanent placement. On the other hand, there will be indirect effects. For example, in the case of children who stem from very disturbed birth families, the fear that 'bad blood will out' could be a cruel burden for many substitute families. Despite this, there is little evidence in the literature to justify such a belief. About forty years ago, Brenner (1951) in a follow-up study of adoptive families showed that pathology in a child's family background had no apparent effect on his development, though it could cause anxiety to the adoptive parents. On the other hand, it is clear that genetic influences can be of relevance, though they will not necessarily be associated with success or failure in outcome. Received opinion and commonsense on this issue has however been challenged by the more recent work of Mednick et al. (1984) who compared the court convictions in Denmark of over 14,000 adoptees with those of their biological and adoptive parents; there was a significant relationship between biological parent criminal conviction and criminal convictions occurring in their children who had been adopted.

The natural family itself is likely to have a bearing on placement outcome where there is involvement in decisions about placements and there is a maintenance of links after placement occurs (Fratter, 1989). Such events illustrate once more the interaction of professional practice, adult attitudes and child responses. The literature relating to parental involvement through access and other links has already been discussed. However, as Triseliotis (1986) suggested, one major challenge now facing adoption workers is to find adoptive families who are willing and able to tolerate contacts between older children and members of their family of origin with whom they already have an attachment. Where commitment exists and agencies are attempting such work, the challenge is proving to be far from impossible (Fratter, op. cit.).

Child variables

For many years there has been a consensus within the adoption literature on the desirability of early placement of children though Pringle (1967) pointed out that it is far from clear whether the crucial factor is the child's age at placement or the diminished likelihood of prolonged 'early deprivation and separation trauma'; the younger the child at placement then the less time there has been for discontinuity in parenting, for multiple placement, etc.. Reich and Lewis (1986), reporting a study of 'hard-to-place' children, suggested that the effects of long periods in institutions make it more difficult for a child to adapt successfully to family life, and that the age of the child has a significant effect on the achievement of permanent placement. By contrast, Tizard (1977) found no correlation between adoption success and the child's age at placement, the children's ages ranging from two to seven-and-a-half years. Whatever may be the explanation for these variations in findings concerning younger children, there can be little doubt that for children placed at older ages, then the likelihood of adoption success diminishes. Thoburn and Rowe (1988) in a recent national study of children with 'special needs' found that 'the only factor which seems clearly and consistently associated with breakdown is age. ... our findings also show that age is a more significant factor than mental or physical disability in predicting placement outcome.'

Such evidence confirms the work of Wolkind and Kozaruk (1986), for example, who reported that the degree of handicap, both physical and mental, was not related to successful outcome. Similarly, Reich and Lewis (1986) argued that possessing a particular physical or psychological health problem does not necessarily mean that the child's ability to manage within a family setting would be affected and that the degree of health or behaviour difficulties were not reflected in the placement outcome in their study. Emotional problems did, however, appear to affect the level of success achieved.

Among other child variables that are important, is gender. In their British study of long-term foster care Rowe et al. (1984), for example, found that boys were more prone to problems, with one in three being disturbed compared with one in five girls. (The same authors also reported no significant differences between the adjustment of white and black youngsters in their sample.)

Finally, the expectations of success will also be shaped to some extent by the degree to which a given child is 'hard-to-place'. Indeed, as has been argued elsewhere, 'it could be that there will always be some children who for one reason or another regrettably are unadoptable and possibly unfosterable, as well as separated from their own families of origin' (Wedge, 1986b). As Thoburn et al. (1986) observed, 'for a proportion of individuals who need permanent placement, adoption will be either inappropriate or impracticable.'

Child-care practice variables

The effectiveness with which tasks are accomplished by professionals could well have effects upon the success of placements. However, detailed studies of child-care practice and their relationship to placement outcomes have not been undertaken. Much work that has been reported concentrates on descriptions of practice and where placement success is examined, the two are not related. Examples include work by Thoburn et al. (1986) referring to 'The Child Wants a Home', by Reich and Lewis (1986), by Argent (1984), and by Sawbridge (1983) in respect of 'Parents for Children' and by Wedge (1986a) in the case of local authority family-finding units in Essex. There are clearly wide differences in practice for family selection - in the length of the selection process, the number of interviews, the involvement of different family members, the use of training groups, and the management of the approval decision - as well as for child selection in terms of the criteria employed in deciding which referrals to accept.

Of course, practice will also vary according to the resource available. It is well documented that placements of children with special needs is an exacting and time-consuming business (e.g. Thoburn et al., 1986; Wedge, 1986a), and there are strong a priori grounds for recognising the importance of professional skill in selecting children and surrogate families, matching where appropriate, managing the placement in the sense of preparing child, family of origin and substitute family, and in the provision of post-placement support as well as, unfortunately, the management of disruption.

With regard to the provision of post-placement support Macaskill (1986) identified the need for both local support from community networks, and for professional help from the specialist agencies themselves. Argent (1988) provided a review of the growing range of post-adoption support services in Britain, operating in both the statutory and the voluntary sector.

Finally, Aldgate and Hawley (1986) argued that placement disruption itself should not necessarily be regarded as failure, particularly where it is well-managed; they present a 12-point checklist for social workers as an aid to practice in this context. They observed that one of the major reasons for disruption is ill-defined access and hence they emphasised the need for workers to define the purpose and frequency of access for birth parents and to ensure that clear agreements are made and upheld by all the parties concerned.

Indicators of success

Assessment of a permanent placement carries a number of pitfalls for the unwary. It is important to be sure about what it is that one wants to measure, and also that the chosen device for measuring it can be consistently applied. Measuring success is further complicated by the need to take account of the situation at the start of placement; this implies a 'before and after' evaluation which is often impossible to achieve in a research study.

Thoburn (1989) made a careful examination of factors used in a wide range of studies to define 'success' in placement. She identified the following eight categories which have been used:

a) Has the placement disrupted? (commonly used)

b) Did adoption actually occur? (e.g. Festinger, 1986)

c) Is there a sense of permanence among the participants? (e.g. Lahti, 1982)

d) Is the child progressing soundly developmentally, both in terms of educational achievement, physical growth and emotional health? (e.g. Seglow et al., 1972; Lambert and Streather, 1980; Rowe et al., 1984).

e) Are there <u>lifetime</u> relationships? (e.g. Triseliotis and Russell, 1984; Thoburn, 1990).

f) Is there a sense of identity? (e.g. Triseliotis, 1980).

g) What is the degree of attachment? (e.g. Hodges and Tizard, 1989).

h) How much satisfaction is there for the various parties? (e.g. Kadushin, 1970; Thoburn et al., 1986).

It can be seen that Thoburn's categories contain many elements which are not absolute, but which depend on relative judgements about progress or degrees of happiness or satisfaction, misery or dissatisfaction. Further, many of the categories depend upon the subjective judgements of adults, children and professionals in reaching a conclusion about the extent to which a placement could be described as successful. On the other hand, objective measures are restricted. It is obviously possible to identify situations where a child has had to be removed from a placement or where an adoption order has been made, and to calculate the duration of a placement. Otherwise, only developmental outcomes are susceptible to objective measurement.

It can thus be seen that 'success' is itself problematic in research, not least because one cannot know in respect of an individual 'what might have been'. The situation is further compounded because one might well obtain different answers at different stages in the placement process according to the duration of time after placement or after adoption, the age of the child, etc..

Finally, reference should be made to the crucial cautionary article by Rowe (1987) in which she discussed the serious problems in interpreting breakdown rates. She analysed the various definitions and terminology as well as the methods of calculating breakdown rates used by different researchers. The article stresses the range of methodologies which have given rise to specific rates of breakdown but which are identifying different characteristics. As Rowe pointed out, 'research which is itself unsound or which is misunderstood or wrongly applied can lead to dangerous dogmatism. And, like all statistics, fostering breakdown rates can be helpful and informative or misleading and confusing.' The same, of course, applies to adoption breakdowns.

3   The study

Given the paucity of research into sibling placement, it was vital in this study to establish some baselines from which further work might be carried out. It was therefore decided to establish the extent to which sibling groups were available for placement and to discover whether they were split up in the process or maintained as an intact group. It seemed important to gather information about children's own backgrounds and characteristics as well as details of social work practice and placement experience. Further, the study set out to explore success in placing the groups of children identified in order to comment on the central issue of whether or not groups should be split. Finally, it was expected that this exercise would indicate avenues for further research which might profitably inform the whole subject area.

Because the study had originally been prompted by concerns of the Eastern Counties Group of Adoption Agencies it seemed appropriate to explore with them ways in which the subject could be pursued. The five agencies concerned covered an area of six counties, providing a range of adoption and long-term fostering services to children with 'special needs'. The children were by definition 'hard-to-place' and as such will have been referred mainly by the local authorities in the area. Of course, the local authorities themselves undertook permanency work and approaches were made to these statutory agencies as well as the voluntary ones for information about the prevalence of siblings being dealt with. The five voluntary agencies willingly volunteered to participate, but the statutory agencies, although also willing, were unable to identify sibling groups in such a way that prevalences could be established, and a sample drawn. The only exception to this was in the County of Essex where computerised records enabled a sample to be identified. However, even here a pilot exercise in one area revealed that sibling groups requiring permanent substitute placement were routinely referred either to one of the voluntary agencies or to one of the County's two Family Finding Units. In the event, therefore, information for this study was obtained from the five voluntary agencies and from the two Family Finding Units operated by Essex Social Services Department.

The sample

In deciding on criteria for inclusion in our sample it was important first of all to discover how many children might be involved. The focus had to be on children referred (rather than, for example, children who had been placed) since it was the outcome of referral that was particularly important. Secondly, it was desirable that records should be reasonably current in the hope that social workers involved might still be in the agency and able to supply information where necessary. Thirdly, however, it seemed important that there should be some children who could have been in their placement for at least three years when our information was gathered so that time could have elapsed to reach beyond the 'honeymoon' period of two years or so identified by Macaskill (1986). Although Macaskill identified the third year of a placement as being particularly difficult for substitute parents, Thoburn and Rowe (1988) found that of the disruptions occurring among children placed in their national sample, 52 per cent occurred within the first year.

Agencies were therefore invited to supply information about the numbers and size of sibling groups on referral at 1st April 1982 or subsequently accepted on referral in the period 1st April 1982 to 31st March 1986. They were also asked to indicate the total number of children on referral over this four year period.

Table 3.1
Children referred: sibling groups and others*

	No. of Siblings	All Referrals	% Siblings
Voluntary Agencies	101	518	19
Statutory Agencies	59	124	48
Total	160	642	25

*On referral on 1 April 1982 or referred for permanent substitute family placement Apr.1982-Mar.1986 - (Eastern Counties).

As Table 3.1 shows this produced a total of 160 children in sibling groups drawn from a total of 642 referrals in all. This means that children in sibling groups comprised 25 per cent of all those on referral to these agencies over the four year period. The Table also shows that the proportion was nearly half in the statutory agencies, but only 19 per cent in the voluntary agencies. The range amongst the individual voluntary agencies was from 9 per cent to 34 per cent, so in no case did it approach the proportion in either of the statutory sector Family Finding Units.

In view of the number of sibling groups it was decided to obtain information on each of them and not to sample from among them. For this purpose, a questionnaire was devised and piloted before being finalised. One of the researchers then visited each agency by arrangement and scrutinised existing records to complete the information on the questionnaire. This was a time-consuming exercise which began in late 1986 and was completed by early summer 1987. This means that any child would by then have been on referral for at least six months and up to five years by the time information was gathered.

It should also be noted that the research was confined to information available in agencies. Most of this was obtained from routine records, though occasionally social workers were asked to clarify specific information which appeared in those records. There was no attempt to interview children, families of origin, or substitute families. Such an exercise was well beyond the scope of the present study, though clearly would be of great value in informing some of the issues which were exposed.

This means that the findings which follow reflect work carried out in the seven agencies and might not be typical of work in other agencies. There is no reason, however, to suppose that in fact it does differ from other specialist adoption and 'permanent' fostering settings. Any idiosyncracies that relate to a specific agency will to some extent be balanced by the policies and practices in the others from which this sample was drawn.

In addition to the usual information about age and sex of the study child, details were obtained about siblings and about the extent of links between the study child and the family of origin; placement history was also recorded as well as social workers' appraisals of placements and details of any breakdown; the age of the substitute mother and previous parenting experience was obtained together with information about the substitute family including the ages of family members; in cases where an initial placement had broken down details were also obtained of any subsequent placement and further substitute families. A list of information gathered for the study appears as an Appendix.

After collection the information was coded and transferred to computer for analysis. In the Tables which follow percentages have been rounded to the nearest whole number with 0.5 rounded upwards. Findings have generally been presented in simplified tables which afford a salient and immediate perspective. However, the structure of data means that simple interpretations can sometimes be misleading. There are two main reasons for this. First, many of the individual children in the study were placed as members of groups; hence some explanatory variables (e.g. age of substitute mother) relate to a group placement where others (e.g. age of child) relate to the individual. In such circumstances, multi-level analysis of the data is required. Such an analysis will form a further development of the work reported here.

Secondly, the occurrence of placement breakdown depends on factors, some of which have been found to interact one with another. In such a situation, significance values based on Chi-square tests on ordinary two-way tables are inappropriate. Hence they are not a routine feature of the presentation which follows. To include them could give a spurious air of credibility to those factors which interact in complex ways. The nature of this interaction between certain key variables is explored in Chapter 6.

4 The children

Among the general population more than 80 per cent of children have at least one sibling and 60 per cent have at least two siblings. This is reflected in the children who enter care. A ten per cent sample survey in one major local authority showed that in the four year period 1981-85, about 82 per cent of children in care had at least one sibling (Wedge and Phelan, 1986). Unsurprisingly, many of the children did not enter care together with their siblings. Millham et al. (1986) found that in their study 45 per cent entered care with one or more siblings. Similarly, Rowe et al. (1984) found that 48 per cent had at least one sibling in care or adopted. Wedge and Phelan's investigation produced a somewhat lower figure. Having examined a 21 per cent sample of children entering care in a four-and-a-half year period in one county, figures showed that 31 per cent of children entered care with at least one sibling, and 15 per cent with two or more siblings.

As already discussed (Table 3.1) the proportion of children being dealt with by the specialist agencies involved in this study and who came from sibling groups was some 25 per cent overall. This suggests that the child care system as a whole tends to deal with individual children to a greater degree than is implied by the proportion of singletons in the population, or by the proportion of children entering care as individuals. This could be quite appropriate in many cases where it is the needs of an individual child of a family which has to be addressed. In other situations, however, it could be that the care system fails adequately to take account of sibling relationships and without due consideration, effectively separates an individual child from other children of the family.

Characteristics of the groups

Table 4.1
Characteristics of the groups

160 children were in 71 groups

56 dyads
13 triads
1 tetrad   (four children)
1 pentad   (five children)

60 full siblings
11 half siblings (at least <u>one</u> half sibling relationship in group).

45 from Voluntary Agencies
26 from Statutory Agencies

By far the majority of the 160 children referred to the agencies in our study were in groups of two. As Table 4.1 shows there were 71 groups in all comprising 56 dyads, 13 triads, one tetrad and one pentad. Sixty of the 71 groups were full siblings and 11 were half-siblings (i.e. at least one of the relationships in the group was of a half-sibling). Forty-five of the groups were referred to voluntary agencies and 26 to the statutory sector. These proportions of sibling groups of varying sizes are not representative of the wider population; fewer of the bigger sibling groups are to be found in children referred than in the population generally or, indeed, in the care of Essex County Council, the authority for whom figures were available to us.

As Table 4.2 shows 58 per cent of the sample were boys - a proportion which corresponds very closely with figures for children in care in Essex, 1981-85 (Wedge and Phelan, op. cit.).

As far as age is concerned, the vast majority of the children were between five and twelve years (71 per cent) and very few were over twelve when accepted on referral. (The oldest child at this point was aged 14 years.) This picture contrasts sharply with the age structure of children in care as a whole. For example, national figures show that at the mid-point of the four years covered by our sample (31.3.84) only 28 per cent of children in care were aged under ten years (DHSS, 1984); this compares with 72 per cent in our sample who were under ten on referral. If the seven agencies studied were to be typical, then very few sibling groups with one child aged 13 or over would be likely to be found on the caseloads of specialist home-finders in either the voluntary or statutory sectors. In this sample, the peak demand is among children who were between their fourth and eighth birthdays on referral.

Table 4.2
Age and gender of children referred
(in completed years of age)

Years	Boys	Girls	Total
0	3	3	6*
1	1	3	4
2	4	1	5
3	5	4	9
4	10	6	16
5	9	7	16
6	10	5	15
7	11	8	19
8	8	3	11
9	9	5	14
10	7	9	16
11	10	4	14
12	2	6	8
13	1	2	3
14	2	2	4
Total	92 (58%)	68 (43%)	160 (100%)

Mean age: 7 years 6 months
*Three pairs of twin babies

Source of referral

Table 4.3
Source of referral of children by sector

	Own County	Other County	London Boroughs*	Total
Voluntary	28	26	47	101
(%)	(28)	(26)	(47)	(100)
Statutory	52	2	5	59
(%)	(88)	(3)	(8)	(100)
Total	80	28	52	160
(%)	(50)	(18)	(33)	(100)

* via BAAF/PPIAS.

Exactly half of the children came from their own County, but this proportion varied dramatically between the statutory and voluntary sectors. Unsurprisingly, 88 per cent of the children placed by the Essex Family Finding Units were referred from that County. Among the voluntary agencies the proportion was only 28 per cent. Nearly half of the referrals to voluntary agencies came from the London

Boroughs via either BAAF or PPIAS. One possible implication of this is that the children referred to voluntary agencies came from further afield, a fact which could be relevant to the maintenance of links with other family members both while on referral and after placement. Unfortunately incomplete information on the records concerning links at the six-month stage after placement precludes any finding about this possibility.

Length of time in care before referral

Table 4.4 shows the length of time spent in care by children before referral to the specialist agencies. Sixty-two per cent had been in care for less than two years, and 18 per cent for four years and over. The Table also shows a clear trend, as would be expected, for the older age groups to have spent longer in care by the time of referral. As many as one-third of 10-14 year olds had been in care for four years or more; but also among this age group, about half had been in care for less than two years.

Table 4.4
Age by length of time in care (pre-referral)

Age on referral		Time in care (years)			
		Under 2	2 + 3	4 + over	Total
0 - 4		34	5	1	40
	(%)	(85)	(13)	(3)	(100)
5 - 9		44	18	13	75
	(%)	(59)	(24)	(17)	(100)
10 -14		21	9	15	45
	(%)	(47)	(20)	(33)	(100)
Total		99	32	29	160
	(%)	(62)	(20)	(18)	(100)

Links with the family of origin

Turning to children's links with their family of origin at referral, just about half of all children had such links. The highest proportion was amongst 10-14 year olds who were members of sibling groups on referral; among these 60 per cent had links at that stage with their family of origin compared with only about 40 per cent in respect of younger children.

Given that more of the older children had been in care for longer, it is perhaps surprising that they were the age group who had most links with their family of origin. Although it could reflect the fact that a fair proportion had been in care for a relatively short time, it does not explain why younger age groups who had spent shorter periods in care were less likely to have links with their family of origin. Perhaps the older children were able themselves to take the initiative more frequently to keep in touch with their original family and were not dependent on their parents alone to be ensuring that a link was maintained; perhaps access was more likely to have been terminated in respect of the younger children. (One reason for this could be that a greater expectation of successful adoption leads to earlier termination of contact based on an unsubstantiated belief by practitioners that the absence of links would enhance its achievement.)

Special needs

By definition all children dealt with by specialist agencies will be children with 'special needs'. In other words, they will fall into that category known as 'hard-to-place'. One of the reasons for defining children in this way is that they are members of sibling groups. However, many of them will also have one or more other special needs. As Table 4.5 sets out, half of the children in the sibling sample had at least one other special need; 14 per cent of them had two or three special needs.

The categories of special need into which the sample fell is also shown in Table 4.5. Given that some children had more than one special need, it is nevertheless interesting to note that it is behavioural and emotional problems which are the most predominant, although black children also figure substantially.

Table 4.5
Recorded 'special needs'

In addition to sibling status:

- 51%   had no other need
- 35%   had one other need
- 10%   had two other needs
- 4%   had three other needs

Of the sample:

- 18%   – behavioural problems
- 14%   – placement needed with black/mixed parent family
- 9%   – emotional problems
- 9%   – enuretic
- 6%   – moderate learning difficulty
- 4%   – speech problems
- 2%   – physically handicapped
- 3%   – other (e.g. epilepsy, hepatitis B)

Indeed, 23 per cent of the referrals to voluntary agencies comprised children needing a placement with a black or mixed family, whereas all of the children with statutory agencies were white. Apart from this difference, voluntary and statutory agency children were very similar in terms of their special needs.

Perhaps not surprisingly, as Table 4.6 shows, more of the older age groups had additional special needs, but even amongst the youngest group the proportion was one in three. Among the older groups the proportion varied but was substantially higher.

It is important to note that so many of the sibling group had other needs because the label 'sibling' could easily distract attention from the other special needs which these children frequently had. This was by no means a sample of 'ordinary' children.

Table 4.6
Age by 'special needs'
(other than 'sibling group')

Age on referral		No special need	At least one special need	Total
0 - 4		27	13	40
	(%)	(68)	(33)	(100)
5 - 9		32	43	75
	(%)	(43)	(57)	(100)
10 -14		23	22	45
	(%)	(51)	(49)	(100)
Total		82	78	160
	(%)	(51)	(49)	(100)

Later in this report the association of categories of special need with disruption is specifically examined. One advantage of the methodology employed is that the assessment of special needs was made before placement and there can be no possibility that where disruption occurs it has been retrospectively ascribed to children with increased numbers of special needs, or with particular categories of special need.

Patterns of sibling-sibling interaction

The decision whether or not to split a sibling group could very well depend on the relationship between siblings. Thus if the pattern of interaction suggests that siblings are unable to tolerate one another's company then that could be, on the face of it, grounds for splitting them. On the other hand if they seem to be very dependent upon one another and to enjoy each other's company that could be a particular reason for maintaining the group - though Forbes (1977) would see that as suggesting that sibling groups should be split. In order to learn about actual practice in this respect, records were scrutinised specifically to learn whether such factors were material to the decision to split or not to split.

The bulk of the data obtained from files related to quasi-parental patterns; thus a child would be described as 'protective', 'bossy' or 'dependent'. This suggests a focus on the nature of the children's relationships with their siblings rather than on the roles played by each child in their family of origin. Indeed, 'roles', e.g. 'takes on function of parent', might be more useful in predicting any likely difficulties in settling into a new family.

The most striking feature of our scrutiny of records was the paucity of information documented about the patterns of interaction. If baby adoptees are excluded, then files relating to one-fifth of the children contained nothing about interaction; for another three-fifths there was hardly any mention; for the further fifth details were included on children as individuals and as members of their birth families. It was notable that the longer a child had been on referral then the greater was the likelihood that details would be documented. Even so, those for whom no comment was available will still have spent an average of five months on referral before being placed.

Where assessments of interaction occurred these could be classified as positive, negative or ambiguous. No obvious relationship was found between these categories and the aim to separate sibling group members at placement. In any event, as is discussed below, almost invariably the aim itself was to maintain the groups, regardless of the pattern of interaction.

Certainly this suggests that as far as information recorded on files was concerned, relatively little attention was given to siblings' interaction with one another; where it was mentioned it had apparently little bearing upon the decision to split or to maintain a given group. In view of the difficulty of adults entering children's worlds and forming a reliable assessment of the extent to which siblings are 'meaningful' to one another, then perhaps this is a wise practice. Anecdotal evidence, however, suggests that in reality this is not a principle upon which practice is based.

As Timberlake and Hamlin (1982) point out, 'in their interactions siblings view one another as individuals with strengths and weaknesses. Each sibling, therefore, adjusts his or her part in an interaction to accommodate the other sibling's part. In other words the involvement of siblings with one another is strongly influenced by the give-and-take of their interpersonal relationships within the close proximity of the family unit and by the life events shared ... the closer the involvement among siblings, the harder it is for an outsider to know what is being reciprocated in sibling interactions.'

5 Placement practices and placement experiences

Regardless of what ultimately happened to sibling groups in placing them in permanent substitute families, a judgement had to be made by the appropriate social workers as to whether the aim should be to maintain the group intact or split the siblings. It seemed important to investigate this question of the aim of placement as well as the actual placement itself since one possibility is that actual placements would be determined to some extent by the availability of homes able to take sibling groups. There could well prove to be a difference between aim and actuality for this reason.

First documented aim

In scrutinising children's records, a note was made of the first documented aim for the sibling group. In practice, in the majority of cases the first aim was to maintain the child with all of its siblings. Table 5.1 shows the extent to which the aim was to maintain, split or splinter sibling groups. 'Splintering' is relevant only to triads and larger groups and refers to situations where a group of siblings is divided in such a way that at least two siblings could be placed together, though not the entire group. Thus, it can be seen that in our sample only one group (of three children) fell into the splintering category. In subsequent analysis these splintered children are included with those who were split.

In the event, the aim to split or splinter sibling groups accounted for about one child in every five. This varied, however, between the statutory and the voluntary agencies,

the former being more likely to be aimed towards split/
splinter. Perhaps this could be accounted for by a
difference of views in the staff of statutory and voluntary
agencies, or perhaps by differences in the children
themselves. We will return to this question below (see
Table 5.4).

Table 5.1
Documented aim: maintain, split or splinter
by sector (children)

	Maintain	Split	Splinter	Total
Voluntary	88	13	–	101
(%)	(87)	(13)		(100)
Statutory	42	14	3	59
(%)	(71)	(24)	(5)	(100)
Total	130	27	3	160
(%)	(81)	(17)	(2)	(100)

Reasons for chosen aims

Table 5.2
Reasons for chosen aims (documented)

	Maintain		Split/Splinter		Total	
		%		%		%
No child related reason given	58	(45)	4	(13)	62	(39)
'Strong bond'	45	(35)	–		45	(28)
Individual needs of child	2	(2)	17	(57)	19	(12)
Views of one child	9	(7)	6	(20)	15	(9)
Limited placement availability	7	(5)	3	(10)	10	(6)
General attitude re undesirability of separating	7	(5)	–		7	(4)
Birth mother's view	2	(2)	–		2	(1)
Total	130	(100)	30	(100)	160	(100)

In scrutinising children's records, a note was also made of the reasons given for the selection of the particular aim, to split or to maintain. Perhaps not surprisingly no child-related reason was given for 39 per cent of the children. There were real differences, however, between those where the aim was to maintain and those for whom it was to split. Thus, no child-related reason was given in respect of almost half of the children whom it was intended should be maintained in their sibling group. Where a reason was given for such children it was very frequently that a 'strong bond' existed between the sibling members. Indeed, this reason was cited in respect of two-thirds of all the children for whom the aim was to maintain and where a reason was given. Other reasons occurred relatively infrequently. Turning to the group of children whom it was aimed should be split, the 'individual needs of the child' was the most common reason given; as Table 5.2 shows this reason occurred for 57 per cent of the children in this group.

There are several other interesting conclusions to be drawn from Table 5.2. First, the views of the child were apparently material to the placement aims of only 7 per cent of the 'maintained' children compared with 20 per cent of the children where the aim was to split the group. To what extent, then, are children's views actually sought? What happens when a child wants or needs to be in a placement separate from another sibling, but that sibling wants or needs to be in a maintained group? Are children given the option of being placed on their own with the opportunity of retaining links with their sibling(s) placed within an accessible geographical range? If, indeed, children's views were material to the chosen aim, then the records failed to mention this fact. Indeed, where the aim was to split the group then a reason was almost always to be found in the record, by contrast with those children where the aim was to maintain the group. These differences suggest that workers involved in dealing with referred sibling groups assumed that the normal practice would be for the group to be maintained. Certainly, this was the more common aim, as we have seen, and perhaps this is why reasons for the chosen aim were frequently not cited. It seems that where the aim was to split the group then such an intention was much more likely to warrant justification in the record.

Given the likely importance of siblings' interaction with one another influencing the aim of the placement, this question was specifically explored. It was found that whether the patterns of sibling interaction were assessed as negative or positive, then the aim was equally likely to be to maintain the group. On the evidence of this small sample, the aim of the placement is not associated with the way brothers and sisters get on together.

Additionally, those children were noted where the record referred to an alternative option in the placement aim. Such evidence was found in respect of only 17 per cent of the relevant children (27 in total). Options were relatively more likely to be mentioned where the first aim was to split rather than to maintain. The reasons given for this are informative. In the cases of ten of the 19 children for whom the first aim was to maintain, and an option was expressed, doubts centred on placement availability; among the children for whom the aim was to split, the aim 'maintain' was rejected because it would fail to meet the individual needs of the children concerned. This finding also is indicative of a wide assumption that siblings should be placed together. Such an aim was rarely queried in the records. Where this did occur, the focus was on the child as an individual.

Prime movers in setting aims

Of course, the chosen aims could very much reflect agency policy, determined by management committees or senior staff. Alternatively, it could reflect the views of individual workers making relatively independent judgements.

On exploring this in children's records, a clear pattern emerged; the child's Social Services Department of origin dominated the situation and their viewpoint was most often expressed and followed in placement aims. It seems that in effect sibling groups were referred by their home social worker to the specialist agency specifically for joint placement. Thus, the specialist agency workers' views were mentioned for only 15 per cent; compared with this, the home Social Services Department's viewpoint was expressed in 95 per cent of cases.

If the referral tended to be 'for a joint placement', then there is, in theory, no reason why the agency workers should be diffident in querying this, if appropriate. The referral itself could be declined where there was unease on the part of agency staff. Does it tend not to occur because specialist agencies are passive? This seems out of character in staff who value their independence. Perhaps, on the other hand, they tend to agree with the judgement of the home social worker and feel no need to record their own views in most cases. Perhaps it is also relevant that some splitting and splintering will have already been effected by the home Social Services Department before children are referred to the specialist agencies. Whatever the reason, it is true that the home social workers will have had an opportunity to assess the children and to weigh the pros and cons of the different options before even approaching the specialist agency. That the approach when made comes in the form of a request for a joint placement could well mean that agency workers are not in a position to query the request for a joint placement with any degree of confidence.

First permanent placements

One measure of the success of the specialist agencies in dealing with sibling groups is indicated by the extent to which placements were found for children. In the event, of the 160 referrals, 133 children were placed in substitute families and a further eight were returned to their family of origin. Thus, only 12 per cent of the children were not placed by the agency concerned. This indicates a broad measure of success on the part of the specialist agencies in finding families for children who were regarded as 'hard-to-place'. Given that such a high proportion of the children also experienced other special needs, it is a considerable achievement on the part of the placers. One difficulty for social workers, however, is the time taken in achieving placements.

Length of time on referral

There was a wide variation between agencies in the average time the children were on referral before being placed. The shortest was less than two months and the longest in excess of nine months. It is clear that families were ready and waiting for some of the children at the time of acceptance on referral. Not surprisingly waiting times of months rather than weeks occured for the majority while agencies searched for suitable homes for these children. Table 5.3 shows that well over half of them had been placed within six months of referral, a time which in the circumstances could be considered relatively short.

Table 5.3
Length of time on referral before first placement

	Number	%	Cumulative %
Up to 3 months	50	36	36
Over 3 months and up to 6 months	32	23	58
Over 6 months and up to 9 months	30	21	79
Over 9 months and up to 12 months	5	4	83
Over 12 months	24	17	100
Total	141*	100	

* includes 'restored' children

Of these 141 placements, 124 (88 per cent) involved children who were maintained in their group and 17 (12 per cent) who were split from their brothers and sisters. Discounting the children who were not placed, the proportions maintained and split (88:12) show a greater tendency towards maintaining than did the aim for placing the children (81:19) (Table 5.1, above).

Type of placement

As Table 5.4 shows children placed by the statutory agencies were apparently more likely to be split from their brothers and sisters. This is very much in line with the aims (discussed above). In fact, the difference would be entirely consistent with voluntary agencies being 'commissioned' on referral to maintain most of the sibling groups referred to them, and for them to accept this as their task.

Table 5.4
Type of placement by agency sector

	Maintain	Split/Splinter	Total
Voluntary	82	8	90
(%)	(91)	(9)	(100)
Statutory	42	9	51
(%)	(82)	(18)	(100)
Total	124	17	141
(%)	(88)	(12)	(100)

Where children remain on referral but there is little sign of a substitute family materialising for a sibling group, there could be a temptation for the agency to seek a good 'holding' placement perhaps in a bridge family or to split the children in order to achieve a quicker placement than would otherwise be the case. Undoubtedly there is a difficult judgement to be made between whether to persist in seeking a family to take a whole sibling group which could be in the child's interest, as against splitting the group but achieving a much earlier placement which could also be in the child's best interest. Deciding what would be the least detrimental course of action with absolute certainty would require an impossible degree of foresight.

Table 5.5
Type of placement by length of time on referral

Time on referral	Type of placement		Total
	Maintain	Split/Splinter	
Up to 6 months	77	7	84
(%)	(92)	(8)	(100)
Over 6 months	47	10	57
(%)	(82)	(18)	(100)
Total	124	17	141
(%)	(88)	(12)	(100)

What actually happened in practice is to some extent indicated by Table 5.5. This shows that of the children on referral for up to six months before placement, only 8 per cent were split. Of those on referral for over six months, 18 per cent were split. Superficially this appears to support the view that there is an association between splitting or maintaining and length of time on referral. It could be that children who are split from their brothers and sisters at placement are those who for whatever reason present particular difficulties in finding a substitute family because of their special needs.

Unplaced children

In all, 19 children were unplaced at the time of our survey, i.e. at least six months and up to five years after the referral.

Whether or not the children were placed was associated with their age at referral. The summary Table 5.6, in which the age range is dichotomized at eight (following the findings of e.g. Thoburn and Rowe, 1988), shows clearly that older children having been accepted on referral were less likely to be placed. Thus, only 4 per cent of under eight year olds were unplaced compared with 21 per cent of those aged eight or over.

Table 5.6
Placed/unplaced by age at referral

	Age at referral (years)		
	Under 8 %	8 and over %	Total %
Unplaced	4 (4)	15 (21)	19 (12)
Placed	86 (96)	55 (79)	141 (88)
Total	90 (100)	70 (100)	160 (100)

[$p < .01$]

However, too much importance should not be read into findings about those who were not placed because among the 19 referred children unplaced, six had been accepted and placed by a different agency. Furthermore, another three children had been placed by the Social Services Department of origin. In other words, of the 19 children who had not been placed following the referral which led to inclusion in this study, nine had been placed by another agency.

Details of the outcome of placement efforts are set out in Table 5.7, from which it can also be seen that of the remaining 10 children only one or two were clearly unlikely to be placed or restored to the family of origin.

The implication of this is quite striking. The system is obviously very successful in finding substitute homes or restoring children to their families of origin, even for the older age groups. Even so, it is clear that individual agencies do find sibling groups containing older children to be the most difficult. The message here for Social Services Departments is that in seeking to make a referral which is proving difficult they should try a range of possibilities or of agencies, or use the clearing arrangements offered by BAAF. The figures show that the voluntary and statutory sections were equally successful in finding and making placements.

Table 5.7
Outcome for 'unplaced' children (N = 19)

Child accepted by more than
one agency and placed by
different agency = 6

Child placed by SSD
of origin = 3

Still awaiting
placement = 5 (1 = child aged 15
 1 = no apparent reason
 3 = restoration being considered)

No longer
on referral = 5 (1 = child wanted residential care
 2 = SSD decided child stay with substitute foster parents and possibly adoption
 2 = introduction failed, restoration being considered by SSD).

Although the 'placing system' is successful overall, there are nevertheless children who were 'technically unplaced' in the sense defined above, i.e. they were not placed in a new substitute family by the agency which had taken them on referral. It seemed important to establish whether there were any particular characteristics of these children which marked them out from those in the 'placed' category. Analysis showed that among children who had been in care up to three years, 10 per cent were unplaced and of those in care for more than three years 15 per cent were unplaced. This means that the time in care was not strongly related to whether children were placed or unplaced, although it will be older children who have been in care the longest.

Similarly, having a 'special need' in addition to being in a sibling group was not related to whether children were placed or unplaced. Further, the first documented aim being to maintain or split was not associated with whether children were placed or not, and similarly the number of siblings in the group was not associated.

To summarize, the only statistically reliable association of whether children were placed or unplaced is the age of the child on referral/acceptance. Those aged eight years and over were five times more likely not to be placed by the agency receiving the referral than children under eight years of age. It should be remembered, though, that other agencies were involved in placing half of the 'unplaced' children. This study, however, is concerned with referrals to given agencies and it is in that context that these analyses are of relevance.

Work with older children presents particular challenges for the child care placement worker. In reviewing evidence from North America, Barth and Berry (1987) write that 'adoption of older children appears to be meeting its promise for children and deserves continued emphasis.' Against this, Triseliotis (1986) and Wedge (1986b) urge arrangements for older children which do not exclude links with the family of origin; each argues that adoption might well not be the most appropriate placement.

Aims and placements

Five sibling groups (13 children) were involved in situations where the first aim was not achieved. Examining these on an individual basis shows that there was no clear single reason for this but a variety of changing circumstances. For example, for a particular group of two siblings the first aim was to split; the older child's introduction to her fosterparents initially went well but then broke down; the younger sibling was being introduced to her own substitute parents and this was progressing well; the agency worker then suggested that the older child might join her sibling and this was, in fact, the outcome.

In another example of a group of three children the first aim was to maintain the group but one child refused to leave residential care; the other two children were jointly placed.

Among another group of three, the first aim was to split the group; the youngest child was the first to be placed, followed by the oldest some five months later; the agency experienced problems in finding a placement for the middle child and thirteen months after the youngest child's placement began, the middle child was placed with the same family.

Placement and disruption

In addition to effectiveness in finding placements for children, another measure of success is the extent to which disruptions are avoided. In this group of children, disruptions amounted to some 21 per cent in all. However, this figure varied only very slightly between those who were split and those who were maintained with their brothers and sisters. Of course, the absolute numbers are quite low and the figures do not suggest any tendency towards a higher degree of disruption in one type of placement as distinct from another. The implications of this will be discussed further below.

Table 5.8
Type of placement by disruption

	Maintain %	Split/Splinter %	Total %
Did not disrupt	91 (78)	14 (82)	105 (79)
Disrupted	25 (22)	3 (18)	28 (21)
Total	116 (100)	17 (100)	133* (100)

*excludes 'restored' children

The new families

Although there was considerable variety in the families which our sample of children joined, there were some interesting characteristics to be found. For example, 65 per cent had a new mother aged 30-39 at placement and for 29 per cent she was aged 40 or over. Sixty-two per cent joined a mother with no previous parenting experience. This is interesting because Berridge and Cleaver's (1987) is the latest report of research which shows the relative advantage when fostering children with special needs of being placed with older and experienced parents. These differences with children in this study will be examined below.

Table 5.9
New families

Study children

Characteristics of new mothers:

65% aged 30-39 at placement
29% aged 40 plus and over at placement
62% had no previous parenting experience

Family composition:

66% - no new step-siblings on placement
13% - one new step-sibling on placement
10% - two new step-siblings on placement
10% - three new step-siblings on placement
2% - four new step-siblings on placement

Where new step-siblings - 60% placed children were youngest
31% placed children were oldest

Of total children -

5% had new step-sib. within 1 year's age
7% had new step-sib. within 1-2 years' age
2% had new step-sib. within 2-3 years' age
20% had new step-sib. with 3 or more years' age gap

As for the children themselves, 66 per cent had no new step-siblings on placement; Table 5.9 shows that a further 13 per cent had one new step-sibling and smaller proportions of children joined larger families. Where there were new step-siblings, 60 per cent of the placed children were the youngest of the family and 31 per cent were the oldest.

It can also be seen from Table 5.9 that where there were new step-siblings, then the bulk of the children were at least three years difference in age from any child of their new family. Placements were unlikely to have been made where there were similarly aged children, though given received knowledge and research stretching back to that of Trasler (1960) and Parker (1966), it is perhaps surprising that as many as 14 per cent of placements involved new siblings who were less than three years different in age from the sample child.

Second permanent placements

In the event, 13 children were placed following the disruption of their first placement. Of these, four were restored jointly to their family of origin and a further two were placed jointly with substitute parents. For seven children a second placement was arranged separate from their siblings, after the first joint placement had been disrupted.

As far as the outcomes of these placements is concerned, there is no record of the children restored to their family of origin. Of the two children jointly placed, one disrupted after 21 months and the other was adopted, apparently successfully. Of the children placed separately, all were 'successful' in that six had been adopted and the seventh was awaiting adoption.

These bare facts suggest that there was a high degree of 'success' in splitting children from their siblings after a joint placement had disrupted. The figures also serve to give a further illustration of the high effectiveness of the total 'placing system' after initial hiccups.

Links between separated siblings

Although there are some gaps in the data recorded on file, it does appear that most of the separated children were maintaining links with their siblings over the first six months of separation. For example, a triad which was splintered exchanged photographs and letters but there was no direct access until one year after separation; a dyad had monthly meetings at each other's new house; another dyad made phone calls, exchanged greetings cards and letters, and although there was no evidence of access this was not precluded. Another splintered triad made visits on occasional weekends; among another splintered triad there were infrequent visits, but the lone child seemed uninterested in maintaining links such that the agency worker recorded that termination might be advisable.

In total, there were 12 groups comprising 29 children who were split or splintered in the first or second placement. Of these, only two groups (5 children) lost links over the first six months of separation and of these two, one re-established links later. Despite this, the vast majority of the links were infrequent or tenuous. There were just two groups (5 children) where the links appeared to be stronger, and in only one group of three children were the links both regularly and frequently exercised.

Whether this degree of contact represents the lack of enthusiasm by substitute parents, prospective new parents, social workers or the children themselves, was not recorded. What must be beyond dispute is that if links are lost, then it is very difficult to restore them because of practical problems in siblings finding one another with the passage of time. On the other hand, if siblings remain in touch with one another even tenuously, there is always the possibility that should children wish it as they get older then those tenuous links could become stronger and serve to meet the needs of the children concerned.

6 The disruptions

Running through this account have been questions about the advantages of one kind of placement over another, the success of placements in which sibling groups are maintained compared with those in which they are split. In an earlier chapter there was discussion of ways in which the success of adoption placements could be measured and in Chapter 2 eight indicators of success were identified (Thoburn, 1990). As was pointed out, many of these measures used in other studies were quite inappropriate for the present exercise since they depended substantially on subjective judgements about a child's satisfaction, happiness, etc. This study has been confined to more objective measures such as whether a child was placed, and, if so, whether the placement disrupted.

Although some readers would be more familiar with the term 'breakdown', reflecting the family's point of view, 'disruption' has been used in this book for the sake of consistency and because it appropriately reflects the child's perspective.

Table 6.1 shows the complete picture for all of the 160 children on referral in the study. Overall, 66 per cent of the referred children were placed in substitute families and had not disrupted by the time our information was obtained. (Nine months to 57 months after placement). Another 5 per cent of the children were restored to their family of origin and about 18 per cent of the total group disrupted. This figure is slightly misleading because 12 per cent of children were unplaced, as described above. Of the placements in permanent substitute families, 21 per cent broke down.

Table 6.1
Outcomes of referral by sector

	Voluntary		Statutory		Total	
	n.	(%)	n.	(%)	n.	(%)
Main Sample (Placed - no disruption)	69	(68)	36	(61)	105	(66)
Unplaced	11	(11)	8	(14)	19	(12)
Restored	6	(6)	2	(4)	8	(5)
Disrupted	15	(15)	13	(22)	28	(18)
Total	101	(100)	59	(100)	160	(100)

Undoubtedly, this is a crude measure of the success or failure of placements. Nevertheless, it is the 'bottom line' definition frequently used by social workers themselves though not without definitional problems of its own (see Rowe, 1987) as also discussed above. Whatever the precise meaning understood by researchers and practitioners, there can be little doubt, however, that the experience for the children and families involved can be extremely traumatic and, for the children, can bring a particularly unwelcome pain in which the distress of the breakup itself is exacerbated by the knowledge that yet another family situation has involved unpleasantness and rejection of some kind.

The overall rate of 21 per cent in our sample is a figure which varies between the agencies, being lower among the voluntary agencies. The overall figure compares closely with that found in the national survey of 'special needs' children referred to voluntary agencies (Thoburn and Rowe, 1988). In their study of the outcomes of placement for 1,165 children, the overall disruption rate was 21.5 per cent. This figure covered a minimum length of time after placement of some 18 months and a maximum of about five-and-a-half years. Thus in the national study there was a greater exposure to risk of disruption by the children involved than in our study. However, Thoburn and Rowe (op. cit.) also show that more than a quarter of all disruptions occur before the end of six months and just over half within the first year after placement. This evidence suggests that in our much smaller and more local sample there could eventually be more disruptions than had taken place by the time our data were gathered but that the order of magnitude is very much in line with the national picture.

Before examining disruptions in more detail, it is important to stress that 'success' in agency terms depends not only on the skill of the workers and the availability and commitment of substitute families; it also depends very much upon which children are accepted on referral, and which are not. All of the agencies under discussion took children with 'special needs' who were by description 'hard-to-place'. If an agency chose to take children who were in the event easier to place, then it is to be expected that their disruption rate would be lower. This is not to suggest that agencies as a matter of policy take the more difficult or the less difficult children on referral; it is intended to illustrate the difficulty of interpreting simple statistics like those referring to disruption rates. There is also the question of how many and which children are unplaced; a further dimension to this is the need to take into account also what happens to children whose placement breaks down and whether they are placed with another family or by a different agency.

Disruption and age on referral

Table 6.2
Disruption by age on referral

Age of child	Did not disrupt	Disrupted	Total
0 - 2	13	2	15
(%)	(87)	(13)	(100)
3 - 5	32	7	39
(%)	(82)	(18)	(100)
6 - 8	32	9	41
(%)	(78)	(23)	(100)
9 - 11	22	9	31
(%)	(71)	(29)	(100)
12 - 14	6	1	7
(%)	(86)	(14)	(100)
Total	105	28	133
(%)	(79)	(21)	(100)

As we have seen, the breakdown rate for children with 'special needs' who are in sibling groups in this study, compares closely with the national figure for breakdowns in all children with 'special needs'. If, however, there is a distinctive sibling dimension then some of the characteristics associated with disruption in the broader sample might apply differently in our sample of siblings. In this connection, the national study found that increasing age of child is closely associated with increased risk of disruption (Thoburn and Rowe, op. cit.) In the national sample, the disruption rate among children placed under the age of nine was 11 per cent, and that among children placed when aged nine and over was 37 per cent. The comparable figures among our sibling groups (Table 6.2) are 19 per cent and 26 per cent, a much reduced difference although the average rate is much the same. This apparent anomaly among siblings is specifically explored further in the latter part of this Chapter.

Reasons for disruption

In scrutinising records for this study, particular attention was given to the circumstances surrounding disruption where this occurred. Six categories of reason were identified.

1) Attachment: failure of child or parents to attach; child unable to integrate into family.

2) Behaviour: child's behaviour unacceptable to substitute parents.

3) Mismanagement: agency worker/SSD failings; poor preparation, lack of post-placement support.

4) Conflict of loyalties: stress in meeting needs of new children and foster parents' own children.

5) External factors: links with family of origin; child wanting to be with a sibling who had already left placement.

6) Other.

To some extent there is the possibility of overlap between these categories. For example, the failure of attachment or the integration of a child into a family could be because of a child's unacceptable behaviour, and could find expression as a conflict of loyalties for the substitute family. When scrutinising records and allocating breakdowns to these categories account was taken of the terms in which the disruption was explained so that the allocation reflects reasons as expressed in the records themselves.

Table 6.3
Reasons for disruption

		% of 28
Attachment failure	11	39
Behaviour	13	46
Mismanagement	10	36
Conflict of loyalties	5	18
External factors	4	14
Other	2	7

<u>N.B.</u> 45 reasons for 28 child disruptions

Table 6.3 shows the reasons for disruption in the sample as a whole. All explicit reasons were included for purposes of analysis and so there is overlap between categories. The

table shows that 'behaviour' was mentioned as a factor in 46 per cent of the disruptions; a failure to attach was mentioned in 39 per cent. Mismanagement of one kind or other by agencies or individual workers was mentioned in 36 per cent of the disruptions, a figure which gives cause for concern; even where it reflects an element of disappointed families projecting their own feelings of inadequacy on to professionals involved, or the unrealistic expectations which some families could very well have possessed, it is nevertheless a figure to disturb any residual complacency among professionals involved in this process.

One of the difficulties in defining 'disruption' arises because quite often a breakdown in a placement can be anticipated, and planned removal of a child from one family and re-placement in another can be accomplished with a minimum of upheaval for all parties concerned. The circumstances of the 28 disruptions among our sample are shown in Table 6.4. For 16 of the children the breakdown was expected and time was available for planning the removal of the children. For the remaining 12 children the breakdown was unexpected and there was limited time to plan. Indeed, five of the breakdowns came quite unexpectedly. Seven were unexpected but the problems which eventually caused the breakdown had been recognised so that there was some time available to work on resolving them.

Table 6.4
Expectation in disruptions

Expectation

Expected, time to plan   16

Unexpected, no time to plan   12

Of these 12 — 5 completely 'out of blue'
                7 presented problems previously
                recognised and there had been
                time to work on resolution

The sibling dimension in disruptions

Table 6.5
Association of sibling factors in disruptions

Closely associated   10
Slightly associated   5
Unassociated   13

The sibling factor cuts across the six categories of reason for breakdown identified above. Also, the sibling factor was important to varying degrees. For ten children it was closely associated with the disruption, and for a further five there was a slight association. For the remaining 13 children the sibling factor appeared not to be associated with the breakdown. (Table 6.5).

Table 6.6 shows the detailed reasons for the 15 children where there appeared to be a sibling dimension to the disruption.

Table 6.6
Nature of sibling factor in disruptions

Close association (N = 10)

Sibling group - strain on family resources (parental care 4; finances 3)	7
Child wanted to join sibling who had left	2
Substitute parents' view - child should be with sibling	1

Slight association (N = 5)

Child jealous of attention given to sibling	1
Substitute parents resented child, viewed as inhibiting growth of their relationship with sibling	1
Three siblings behaved competitively and violently towards each other	3

The largest group comprised those siblings who caused a strain on the family resources which proved intolerable. Among the seven children involved, four broke down because of demand on parental care as such, and three for financial reasons. There were three siblings in one group whose behaviour towards one another could not be contained. Finally, in five cases there were relationships between the siblings which suggested that either they should be together rather than separated, or vice versa. The desired movement was not all in the same direction.

Putting these details in a broader context, and assuming that placements which did not break down were satisfactory (and that is an assumption which begs a major question) then the sibling dimension was a factor contributing to an unsatisfactory placement in only 11 per cent of all the 133 individual situations, perhaps an unexpectedly low proportion. This is not to say that none of these particular 15 placements would have broken down had there not been a sibling dimension. Nevertheless, it is important to note that although there were situations where tensions were greater because siblings had been placed together and the group maintained, there were also difficulties arising because children had been split from a sibling and wished to be reunited. The implication overall, then, is that placement agencies seem generally not to have failed children in sibling groups either when maintaining them or when splitting them. On the whole, most placements worked out satisfactorily; among those which did not, over 40 per cent involved no sibling dimension; where there was a sibling dimension then the move could be in either direction, from maintained or from split situations.

Taking the information a little further, we have seen that some sibling groups presented difficulties in placement and that individual children sometimes left them. In total, eight children were left behind in such circumstances. Of these two were assessed as having 'less-than-successful' placements; the other six were successful.

It was the general pattern that where placements broke down and more than one child was involved, then all children tended to leave at the same time. Where this did not occur then the younger child left first.

Before leaving the sibling dimension, it should be noted that, of course, there could well be an effect on placements succeeding (i.e. not disrupting) because siblings are located together. Evidence of this is not available from the present study, but Thoburn and Rowe (1988) found that the placements of children aged between 5 and 8 years were less likely to break down where siblings were placed together rather than where children were placed alone.

Factors associated with disruption

Given that placement disruption is the 'bottom line', and brings so much pain and distress in its wake, it is important to explore the circumstances in which it occurs, both to seek to improve practice and hence to avoid disruption in cases where difficulties became apparent, and also to ensure that wherever possible placements which are made are those which are least likely to break down.

Identifying appropriate practices and determining characteristics of child and substitute family which will minimise placement breakdown has been the subject of relatively little research. Much that has been written to date relies on anecdotal evidence or received professional views. Donley (1978) held that adoption disruption occurs because of one or more of three circumstances:

1. critical factors unidentified by worker or family in their early efforts together;

2. mis-assessment of the capacity or readiness of family or child to make an adoptive attachment;

3. unpredictable circumstances which preclude the normal progress of the adoption.

These ideas have been much quoted and utilised in the adoption and fostering literature, for example Fitzgerald (1983), and Aldgate and Hawley (1986). Donley's conceptual framework, however, is of relatively little use in the search for ways of anticipating and preventing placement disruption. To take the three circumstances in reverse order, 'unpredictable circumstances' are by definition unpreventable; assessment of the capacity for attachment is a very inexact business and literature has little to suggest how it might be executed reliably; Donley's first circumstance refers to factors which could well be known without their critical importance being appreciated.

Donley's suggestions together with the work of more recent writers, e.g. Aldgate and Hawley (op. cit.), are addressed very much to practice issues, to the way in which information should be shared with adopters or parents providing long-term fostering. The information in our study by contrast lends itself to exploring attributes of the children to be placed and of the new families which were associated in actuality with disruption.

We looked at a whole host of variables and examined the strength of the association between each of them and disruption itself. Of course, no factor necessarily provides an explanation of the disruption; it merely expresses the strength of an association. Table 6.7 includes each of the single variables with an association which reached statistical significance. Identifying these variables is an important stage towards more complex analysis; findings involving single variables must be treated cautiously as, without further exploration, single variables can prove misleading and over-simplistic.

Children with other 'special needs'

About half of the children in our sample had at least one other 'special need' in addition to being members of sibling groups (Table 4.5). Of the children who had such additional needs, 29 per cent eventually disrupted. Among those with no special need other than that of belonging to a sibling group, only 13 per cent disrupted. Looking at this in a different way, it means that of all the children who suffered disruption 68 per cent had at least one other 'special need'. This could suggest that the sibling dimension is relatively unimportant but that where there is a sibling dimension to disruption, then it could be a 'last straw' effect, i.e. one which when taken with all the other difficulties inherent in particular situations proves more than can be coped with.

Behaviour problems

Behaviour problems figured largely in the 'special needs' which our sample of children presented (Table 6.3). Also, behaviour problems featured in nearly half of all the breakdowns. Table 6.7 shows the relationship of behaviour problems as a 'special need' on referral with disruption of the subsequent placement. The placements of 40 per cent of the children with a behaviour problem disrupted subsequently, as against 17 per cent of those without a behaviour problem. Of all children whose placements disrupted, 36 per cent had had behaviour problems beforehand.

Table 6.7
Individual factors associated with disruption

	Did not disrupt	(%)	Disrupted	(%)	Total	(%)
No other special need	58	(87)	9	(13)	67	(100)
Other special need	47	(71)	19	(29)	66	(100)
No behaviour problem	90	(83)	18	(17)	108	(100)
Behaviour problem	15	(60)	10	(40)	25	(100)
Up to 18 months in care	55	(87)	8	(13)	63	(100)
Over 18 months in care	50	(71)	20	(29)	70	(100)
Up to 3 months on referral	42	(88)	6	(13)	48	(100)
More than 3 mths. on referral	63	(74)	22	(26)	85	(100)
Substitute mother aged under 35	51	(88)	7	(12)	58	(100)
Substitute mother aged 35 or over	54	(70)	21	(28)	75	(100)
None or one new step-sibling	89	(85)	16	(15)	105	(100)
At least two new step-siblings	16	(57)	12	(43)	28	(100)
No previous parenting experience	70	(85)	12	(15)	82	(100)
Some previous parenting experience	35	(69)	16	(31)	51	(100)

Time spent in care

Length of time in care varied considerably across our sample. Those children in care for the longest periods could be those who presented the most difficulty to workers in planning for their future, those whose care histories were fraught with indecision, changes of mind, periods of return to the family of origin, multiple moves, and, no doubt, for some children 'drift' in care. Table 6.7 shows that 29 per cent of the children who had been in care longer than 18 months at the referral/acceptance point, suffered disruption compared with 13 per cent of those who had been in care for 18 months or less. Strikingly, of all the children whose placements disrupted, 71 per cent had been in care for more than 18 months. In the sample as a whole, 53 per cent of the children had been in care for this period.

Time on referral before placement

There was a wide variation in the length of time that children spent on referral before being placed (Table 5.3). Table 6.7 indicates that this was associated with disruption. Thus, 26 per cent of the children who had been on referral awaiting placement for longer than three months suffered disruption compared to 13 per cent of those who had been on referral for three months or less. Indeed, as many as 79 per cent of all the children who suffered disruption had been on referral awaiting placement for more than three months; this compares with 64 per cent of the total placed children who had been on referral for more than three months.

Age of substitute mother

Researchers generally have been interested in the importance of age of substitute parents to the outcome of substitute family placements. Berridge and Cleaver (1987) found that fewer breakdowns were associated with foster mothers over the age of 40. Evidence from the present study differs from those findings in this respect. As Table 6.7 shows, 28 per cent of the children with new mothers who were aged 35 and over, suffered disruption; this compares with 12 per cent of the children whose new mothers were under 35 at the time of placement.

Overall, 75 per cent of the children who experienced disruption were with new mothers who were aged 35 or over; this compares with 56 per cent among all children who were placed with mothers of this age range. Because this evidence is opposite to that of Berridge and Cleaver in respect of long-term fostering, it is perhaps useful to illustrate the trend in disruption rates between children placed with mothers who were aged in their 20s, their 30s, and their 40s, respectively. The rates were none, 19 per cent and 42 per cent. This finding is explored below.

Presence of new siblings

Again, a factor known to be associated with success in placement has been the presence of other children in the family and their age relative to the child placed. In our sample and taking each factor individually, age of other children proved not to be significant, but the presence of two or more new siblings was a factor. Thus, disruptions occurred among 43 per cent of the children placed with at least two new step-siblings, but only 15 per cent of those where there was one or no existing children. Overall, the same proportion, 43 per cent, of study children who suffered disruption had two or more new step-siblings.

Previous parenting experience of new parents

As Table 6.7 also shows, study children placed with new parents who already had some parenting experience were more likely to suffer disruption. This finding is also in contradiction to that of Berridge and Cleaver (op. cit.) who established that there were fewer breakdowns in their sample where foster parents had previous experience of parenting.

Among children in our sample disruption was experienced by 31 per cent of those placed with new parents who already had some parenting experience; this compares with 15 per cent of those placed with new parents who had had no previous parenting experience. Of the children whose placements broke down, 57 per cent were with parents who had previous parenting experience; among all our sample the proportion was 38 per cent.

The extent to which this finding reflects age of substitute mother and presence of other step-siblings will now be explored further along with other possible overlapping factors.

Anomalous findings

The analysis of factors associated with disruption has revealed two problems so far. First, taking each of the factors individually is less than satisfactory. For example, in the findings (Table 6.7) significantly different rates of disruption were associated with each of the variables "older substitute mother", "some previous parenting experience", and "having at least two new step-siblings". The older substitute mothers, however, will be more likely to have had previous parenting experience, and children joining homes where their mother has some previous parenting experience would be very likely to join one or more new step-siblings. Similarly, having a behaviour problem at the time of referral was associated with a greater risk of placement breakdown, as was having any other special need. It is clear, however, that children with no other special need will not have a behaviour problem at the time of referral so there is an overlap between these two categories.

A second reason for concern about the findings relating to disruption is that some of the individual factors, which appear to be related, could well be merely surrogate characteristics. It could be, for example, that it is the age of the mother rather than the presence of new step-siblings or previous parenting experience which is the vital factor in the association with placement breakdown. The need for further investigation is supported by the evidence that a number of these findings do not coincide with other adoption research or work in the related field of fostering placement breakdown. For example, Thoburn and Rowe (op. cit.) in their national study found a clear relationship between disruption and children being older at the time of placement. Such a direct association was not present in our own study. Further, Berridge and Cleaver (op. cit.) found a reduced rate of placement breakdown in substitute families where the mother was older rather than younger; this is the reverse of our own finding. Perhaps, interactions between the variables could explain the differences in the current study from those established by other researchers. This is also explored later in this chapter.

Special needs, step-siblings and disruption

Table 6.8 shows the average number of step-siblings in the substitute family in which children were placed. The calculations are made according to whether or not the placement subsequently broke down, and these in turn are divided to reveal any differences associated with the number of special needs of the child being placed. Thus one can see that among children with no special needs the average number of new step-siblings was 0.5 in placements which did not disrupt, but it was 1.0 in families where placement disruption occurred. At the other extreme, among children with two or three special needs there was on average 0.6 siblings in placements where no disruption took place, but 1.0 where disruption did occur.

Table 6.8
Average number of step-siblings by number
of special needs and disruption

Number of special needs	Did not disrupt		Disrupted	
	Step-siblings		Step-siblings	
0	0.5	(29/58)	1.0	(9/ 9)
1	0.6	(19/34)	1.5	(17/11)
2, 3	0.6	(8/13)	1.0	(8/ 8)

It seems clear from Table 6.8 that there is a much higher frequency of step-siblings in those families where disruption occurred compared with those where it did not. What is also striking from Table 6.8 is that the number of special needs itself is of little relevance. Given the apparent importance of "number of new step-siblings" it seemed best to pursue this particular line of enquiry.

New step-siblings

Of course, many of the study children were placed in families where there was no new step-sibling at all. As Table 6.9 shows, of the 133 children placed, 88 (66 per cent) fell into this category; only 45 of the study children (a third of the total) were placed in families where there was at least one new step-sibling. Table 6.9 shows the rate of disruption among these two groups of children. It can be seen that where there was no new step-sibling, the placements of some 16 per cent of the children had broken down; where there was a new step-sibling then this proportion increased to 31 per cent. However, even in these situations about 7 out of every 10 children placed did not disrupt. Clearly, having step-siblings could be associated with placement disruption in particular circumstances and, given the findings of other researchers mentioned above, it was important to explore this.

Table 6.9
Disruption by number of new step-siblings

	No new step-siblings	%	One/more new step-siblings	%	Total	%
Did not disrupt	74	(84)	31	(69)	105	(79)
Disrupted	14	(16)	14	(31)	28	(21)
Total	88	(100)	45	(100)	133	(100)

Age structure of children in substitute families

Because the simple analysis covered in Table 6.9, then, could itself hide important factors, the age structure of children in substitute families was examined in more detail.
Of the 45 children who were placed with a step-sibling in their new families, 14 were the oldest of the group, and 27 were the youngest; the remaining four occupied an intermediate position. Among those who were oldest, the disruption rate was 50 per cent. This compares with a disruption rate of 22 per cent for those who were the youngest of their new family.

Table 6.10 shows the numbers of children in these various groups. It also shows the placed children characterised according to the difference in years between their age and that of the new sibling nearest to them in age. There are three groups according to the difference in age, under one year (shown in Table 6.10 as 1), one year and under three years (shown in the Table as 3), and three years and over (shown as 4).

Table 6.10
Study children placed with other children:
Disruption and age factors

Number of new step-siblings	Oldest			Inter-mediate			Youngest			Total
Years difference*	4	3	1	4	3	1	4	3	1	
No disruption										
1	5	–	–	–	–	–	10	–	–	15
2	–	1	–	–	–	–	5	1	–	7
3	–	–	1	–	2	1	2	1	2	9
Disruption										
1	2	–	–	–	–	–	–	–	–	2
2	2	1	–	–	1	–	–	1	1	6
3	1	1	–	–	–	–	–	1	1	4
4	–	–	–	–	–	–	–	1	1	2
No Disruption sub-total	5	1	1	–	2	1	17	2	2	31
Disruption sub-total	5	2	–	–	1	–	–	3	3	14
Total	10	3	1	–	3	1	17	5	5	45

*Years difference: 4 = 3 years and over
3 = 1 year and under 3 years
1 = under 1 year

Table 6.10 shows a noticeable group of 17 children who proved to be the youngest in their new family by at least three years and among whom no disruptions occurred. This suggests that they were a particularly favoured group. Most of them were pairs of sibling children, but in one instance four siblings out of a family of five were included, the eldest having been placed with the other four but being only between one and two years younger than the youngest of the new step-siblings. For the purposes of further analysis, however, this additional child is included in the group of "favoured" children, bringing their total to 18. For the purposes of identification, these children will be referred to as "Group A".

Thus, there are three groups of children now under consideration:

> Group A comprises those placed with one or more new step-siblings, all at least three years older than the study child (n = 17 + 1).
>
> Group B are other children who were placed with one or more new step-siblings but were not the youngest by at least three years (n = 27).
>
> Group C are those children placed without a new step-sibling (n = 88).

Disruption and age at referral

Given the importance attached to child's age at referral and age at placement as a factor contributing to the likelihood of disruption, (see Berridge and Cleaver (op. cit.); Thoburn and Rowe (op. cit.)), it was surprising that when the total sample was considered, no evidence was found of a significant relationship between age at referral and disruption among the children in this study.

Table 6.11
Disruption by age at referral
(Groups A, B and C)

	No Disruption	Disruption	Total
Group A			
Under 8	14	–	14
8 and over	4	–	4
Group B			
Under 8	2	8 (80%)	10 (100%)
8 and over	11	6 (35%)	17 (100%)
Group C			
Under 8	54	8 (13%)	62 (100%)
8 and over	20	6 (23%)	26 (100%)

A possible explanation for this can be seen in Table 6.11. This shows the prevalence of disruption in Groups A, B and C which suggests that the age of children at referral is associated with disruption but that an interaction occurs to cancel out the statistical effects. Thus, in Group A where, as we have seen, no disruptions occurred, 14 of the 18 children were aged under eight. This is not surprising since Group A comprised those children who joined a family where there were already children, but where the placed child was at least three years younger than any of the step-siblings. It follows, therefore, that children in Group A will tend to be relatively young.

In Group B, however, 10 of the 27 children were also under eight and, of these, eight disrupted. They were in families where they joined step-siblings but where the placed child was not the youngest by at least three years. Among children aged eight and over, six of the 17 disrupted. Thus, in Group B, disruption was more common among children under eight than among those who were older than this.

Despite the limited numbers of children involved, the findings are striking. They suggest that older children who are closer in age to their new step-siblings can perhaps prove relatively more resilient and less threatened in their new relationships than younger ones. On the other hand, the younger children could be particularly vulnerable to perhaps rivalrous situations when placed with new step-siblings who are close to them in age. Both the younger and the older children, however, have a high risk of disruption compared with those in Group A or Group C. Indeed, older children in Group C did show the expected greater risk of disruption compared with those under eight years, but disruption proved only slightly more common among them (23 per cent) than among the sample as a whole (21 per cent).

This provides further evidence that a crucial element in the risk of disruption is the presence of new step-siblings coupled with the age gap between them and the placed child. Perhaps this arises because children close to one another in age possess similar needs and make similar demands on their parents; in such a situation the parents themselves might experience greater conflict, particularly if the newly arrived children have additional needs stemming from their separation from the birth family and their consequent experiences. Also, there could be heightened conflict for the children; those established in the family will be in a comparatively assured position when confronted with the new arrival who, in turn, might feel compelled to compete in an inappropriate and counter-productive fashion. Should difficulties between the children be unresolved their parents could be put in the position of having to choose - with the outcome being placement breakdown. In this way the various parties and the several pressures could be interacting to increase substantially the risk of disruption.

It might be postulated that children are best placed in childless families where there can be no step-sibling complication. The current study does not support that. The risk of breakdown is not increased in families where there are pre-existing children when the placed children are younger than any new step-sibling by at least three years.

Previous parenting experience

Comment has already been made about the overlapping of the two factors "previous parenting experience" and "presence of a new step-sibling". Table 6.12 shows that this overlap is almost absolute. As would be expected, in those families in which the 45 study children are placed with new step-siblings, then all of the parents have previous experience. Also, for 82 of the 88 children joining families where there was no new step-sibling, then the parents had no previous experience of that role.

Given the relevance of new siblings and their closeness in age to the placed children, it is obviously best to ignore the parenting experience as a factor associated with disruption. It does, indeed, appear to be in essence a surrogate factor for the presence of new step-siblings and because of this close relationship it is of no independent relevance for this study.

Table 6.12
Presence of new step-siblings by
previous parenting experience

Previous parenting experience	No	Yes	Total
New step-children			
None	82	6	88
One or more	-	45	45
Total	82	51	133

Time in care

The length of time spent in care by children before referral to the placing agencies extended up to seven-and-a-half years. The earlier finding (Table 6.7) showed that on average, the group of children in care for more than 18 months was about twice as likely to experience disruption as the group of children in care for up to that time. Table 6.13 examines these findings further, according to whether the children belonged to Group A, B or C as defined above.

The first notable feature about this Table is that none of the children who were referred after having spent less than three months in care, proved subsequently to be in placements which broke down. Of the 18 children concerned, four were placed in families where there were new siblings and where they were substantially the youngest; 14 were placed in families where there was no new step-sibling. These children, referred after a relatively short time in care, comprise another particularly favoured group in terms of the disruption of the placement.

The second notable finding concerns Group A, the children who were placed with new step-siblings and where they were the youngest by at least three years. It can be seen that these children had been in care for varying periods of time but that only four of them had experienced care for less than eight months; three of the 18 children had been in care for over four years.

Table 6.13
Length of time in care by disruption
(Groups A, B and C)

	Group: A		B		C		Total	
	ND	D	ND	D	ND	D	ND	D
Length of time in care								
3 mos. or less	4	–	–	–	14	–	18	–
Over 3 mos./ up to 8 mos.	–	–	2	–	6	3	8	3
Over 8 mos./ up to 16 mos.	2	–	–	3	20	2	22	5
Over 16 mos./ up to 2 yrs.	9	–	–	2	11	3	20	5
Over 2 yrs./ up to 4 yrs.	–	–	6	5	16	4	22	9
Over 4 yrs.	3	–	5	4	7	2	15	6
Total	18	–	13	14	74	14	105	28

ND – No disruption; D – Disruption.

In the earlier discussion of length of time in care, it was suggested that children who had spent longer periods in care were those who had experienced more changes of placement and were perhaps among the more difficult and damaged children in the sample. It was therefore not possible to assess whether the disruptions occurring in the study children stemmed from the experience of a lengthy period of time in care, or that the more difficult children who were most likely to disrupt in placement were also those who would have spent a long time in care because of the difficulties they presented. A partial answer can be given to this speculation if we can assume that the experiences in care of children in Group A were typical of the sample as a whole. In the light of the small numbers involved idiosyncratic reasons could explain the findings obtained but it is reasonable to suggest that although a long period of time in care prior to referral is more likely to be associated with placement disruption, the specific circumstances of the new family seem to be more important than the child's previous experience in care. This seems to be true even for those children in Group B who were placed in families with new step-siblings but where they were not the youngest by three years or more. Among this group, as has been shown, there was a particularly high rate of disruption (52 per cent), but the rate was no greater among the 20 children who had experienced care for more than two years. It appears that the high rate of disruption among children in Group B is not simply associated with length of time in care prior to referral - although it is notable that among these children 20 of the 27 (74 per cent) had been in care for more than two years.

Age of substitute mother

Children were placed with mothers ranging in age from 23 to 49 years, as Table 6.14 shows.

Table 6.14
Age of substitute mother by disruption
(Groups A, B and C)

Age	Group A		Group B		Group C	
	ND	D	ND	D	ND	D
23	-	-	-	-	2	-
24	-	-	-	-	2	-
27	-	-	1	-	3	-
30	-	-	2	-	5	1
31	2	-	-	3	9	-
32	-	-	1	-	8	-
33	-	-	-	-	6	2
34	4	-	2	1	4	-
35	-	-	2	-	2	-
36	-	-	-	4	6	1
37	2	-	-	2	6	-
38	1	-	2	1	3	1
39	-	-	-	-	4	-
40	-	-	-	-	2	1
41	2	-	-	-	1	4
42	2	-	-	-	4	2
43	-	-	-	-	4	2
44	-	-	-	3	3	-
49	5	-	3	-	-	-
Total	18	-	13	14	74	14

ND = No disruption; D = Disruption.

As far as Group A is concerned it can be seen that the mothers ranged from 31 to 49 years, there being no disruptions amongst these children. Among children in Group C, there is statistically significant evidence that the substitute mothers in placements which broke down tended on average to be older by several years than those where the placement did not break down. Part of this effect can be ascribed to the seven children in Group C with young substitute mothers aged 23, 24 and 27 (seven children placed with three mothers) none of whom was involved in a placement which broke down.

In Groups A and B, where by definition there are new step-siblings in the permanent substitute family, there is a tendency towards older mothers. This is to some extent influenced, as well as exemplified, by the eight children (five plus three) placed with two mothers aged 49. Of these eight children, only two were without a special need (additional to their sibling group membership); of the other six, three were black children, two had behaviour difficulties, two were eneuretic, one was epileptic, one "educationally sub-normal", and one had a speech problem (i.e. there were ten additional special needs among these six children). Given such evidence as well as the general finding about the age of substitute mothers, it seemed worth exploring whether there were indications that children with additional special needs were placed with older substitute parents in case the increased risk of disruption was associated with the additional special needs rather than mother's age.

Table 6.15 shows the mean age of mothers and the number of special needs in children in Group C, i.e. children placed in families where there were no new step-siblings and where the statistically significant association between disruption and maternal age was found. From Table 6.15 it can be seen that the average age of the mothers of children with two or more additional needs, or with one additional need, was not appreciably different from that of the mothers where there were no special needs; this obtained both where the placement did not break down and where it did. In essence, the evidence here is that the number of special needs is irrelevant and is not an explanation of the increased disruption rate where older substitute mothers were involved.

Table 6.15
Mean age of mothers by disruption and
number of special needs in children
(Group C)

No. of needs	Did not disrupt			Disrupted		
	None	One	Two+	None	One	Two+
N.	40	25	8	6	3	5
Mean Age	35.5	33.2	34.7	39.2	38.7	38.6

Child's age, special needs and behaviour problems

Earlier in this chapter differences were found in the association of child's age at referral with disruption according to the composition of the family in which the child was placed (i.e. Group A, B or C.) In the light of this it seemed important also to explore the association with disruption both of the number of special needs (and of behaviour problems in particular) and to take into account child's age.

Table 6.16 shows the children in Groups A, B and C according to age group of child, whether there were additional special needs, and whether disruption occurred or not. (This Table excludes the three sets of twins who were referred very shortly after birth because in the context of this analysis they comprise an anomalous group.) Again ages are grouped at under or over 8 years of age because of findings in other studies which link a variable risk of disruption with these age categories (Thoburn and Rowe, 1988).

Table 6.16
Additional 'special needs' and age group by disruption
(Groups A, B and C)

	Aged under 8 years		Aged 8 and over		Total*
	Did not disrupt	Disrupted	Did not disrupt	Disrupted	
Group A					
No needs	7	0	2	0	9
Needs	4	0	3	0	7
Total	11	0	5	0	16
Group B					
No needs	1	3	5	0	9
Needs	1	4	6	7	18
Total	2	7	11	7	27
Group C					
No needs	24	6	13	0	43
Needs	26	2	7	6	41
Total	50	8	20	6	84

* Excludes three pairs of twin babies

It has already been shown (Table 6.11) that there are particularly high levels of disruption among children in Group B - i.e. in substitute families with a new step-sibling but where the placed child was not younger than the step-sibling(s) by at least three years. Table 6.16 shows that despite this high disruption rate overall, there were no disruptions among the five children with no additional special needs who were aged eight years or more. The numbers are small but the finding is supported by evidence from children in Group C - i.e. placed in families without a new step-sibling. Here again there were no disruptions among the 13 children with no special needs and aged eight years of age or more. Among these older children there is a high rate of disruption where additional special needs were present.

Although there are these concentrations of disruption, the absence of disruption is found at all ages, sometimes with and sometimes without the presence of additional special needs. The same situation is found when the 25 children with behaviour problems are specifically examined (Table 6.17). The exception to this is that no disruption occurred in any of the six placements involving a child aged under five and with a recorded behaviour problem. Apart from this, among children with a recorded behaviour problem, disruption (and non-disruption) occurred throughout the age range; there was no association between age at referral and disruption among these 25 children with a behaviour problem.

Table 6.17
Age (in complete years) by placement disruption
(Group A, B and C)
Children with a behaviour problem

Age	Group A		Group B		Group C	
	ND	D	ND	D	ND	D
2	1	-	-	-	1	-
3	1	-	-	-	2	-
4	-	-	-	-	1	-
5	1	-	-	1	2	1
6	-	-	-	1	1	-
7	1	-	-	-	1	1
8	-	-	-	-	-	1
9	-	-	-	1	1	1
10	-	-	-	2	-	-
11	-	-	-	-	1	-
12	-	-	-	-	-	1
13	-	-	1	-	-	-
Total	4	-	1	5	10	5

ND = No disruption.   D = disruption

Tables 6.16 and 6.17 show that children with special needs additional to their membership of a sibling group (and also the specific sub-group of those with a recorded behaviour problem) were found in each of the Groups A, B and C; this holds broadly true for children under eight and those aged eight years and over. Table 6.15 has shown that additional needs are not generally related to an increased risk of disruption and this remains substantially true when the two age-groups are considered for each placement group (A, B and C). Table 6.18 (from which the six infant twins have again been excluded) indicates that of the 66 children with additional special needs 62 per cent were placed in families where there were no new step-siblings (42 per cent younger and 20 per cent older children); these proportions closely matched those for the sample as a whole (66 per cent, 46 per cent and 20 per cent respectively). Given the relatively small numbers involved there is a surprisingly similar pattern of matched proportions in Groups A and B, although there is a suggestion that disproportionately slightly more of the older children with additional needs are placed in Group B (i.e. in families where there were new step-siblings and the placed child was not younger by at least three years).

Table 6.18
Children having additional special needs
by placement group within age groups
(percentaged*)

	No additional special needs	Additional special needs	Whole Group
Group A			
Under 8	13	6	9
8 and over	2	5	3
Group B			
Under 8	8	8	8
8 and over	7	20	13
Group C			
Under 8	49	42	46
8 and over	21	20	20
	100 (n = 61)	100 (n = 66)	100 (n = 127)

*Excluding 3 pairs of twin babies

The major implication of Table 6.18 is that there is no tendency for children with additional special needs to be placed disproportionately in families which are childless or where there are already children. The same held for children with a behaviour problem. Such factors can thus be disregarded when interpreting the more striking findings concerning placement group, substitute mother's age, etc..

The most important variables

At this stage in analysing these data, no special and remarkable features were identified concerning the length of time on referral, or children's links with their family of origin at referral. These variables, however, were included in a fuller analysis. The details of this, together with a further analysis using multi-level modelling, will be described elsewhere (see Lewis and Wedge, in preparation). It initially included all of the variables mentioned in this Chapter and identified as of relevance in their association with disruption. The more detailed analysis excluded children in Group A and the children placed as babies, and involved 111 of the children placed in substitute families.

The factors which were included comprised: number of new step-siblings; age-difference between placed child and new step-sibling closest in age; whether placed child older or younger than step-siblings; child's age at referral; time on referral; time in care prior to referral; links at referral with adults in the family of origin; links with a sibling who was not a member of the group originally referred for placement; age of substitute mother at time of placement; and, as the variable to be explained, whether the placement disrupted or not.

The most important findings concerned the crucial importance of three factors for this group of children. First, the age of the mother continued to be associated with disruption. Secondly, the time spent on referral to the agency was also associated with disruption such that the more time spent on referral then the higher the risk that disruption would occur. The third factor concerned length of time in care and its relationship with children's links with the family of origin at the time of referral; the analysis showed that if links with the family survived then the magnitude of the length of time in care was not associated with disruption; on the other hand, if links with the family of origin had been broken then the magnitude of the length of time in care was associated.

This is a particularly important finding in view of the evidence from psychological research discussed in Chapter 2 above, which stresses the relevance of relationships with members of the family of origin, including siblings. It suggests that the increasing trend towards access of family members to children in care needs to be further developed and extended if placements in substitute families are to be as successful as possible, and if children are to acquire and retain the self-identity which is a crucial component in healthy emotional development.

If to these variables (age of substitute mother, time spent on referral, and time in care/links with family of origin) one adds findings relating to the age of the child placed relative to any new siblings, then the major factors associated with disruption become clear. Notably they are factors which in many instances could be varied by agency and social worker practice.

The importance of these and other findings from the study are discussed in Chapter 7.

7 Overview on work with sibling groups

Like many research undertakings the project reported here has prompted many new questions which can only be answered by further, more detailed research. This is hardly surprising in an area of investigation which, as we have seen, has received hardly any attention. Indeed, it is not just the placement of siblings about which there is so much ignorance; the relevance of sibling relationships to human development is itself a largely unknown subject. Hence, it is easy to envisage perhaps a further twenty years of research by psychologists and others enquiring into child development before sibling relationships can be appropriately understood. Only as new understandings emerge can social workers and others involved in the placement process know how best to meet the interests of children in sibling groups.

Given such a state of ignorance, the findings from this relatively small-scale study of the placement of sibling groups offer considerable encouragement. This brief overview will set out some of the key findings.

Numbers of sibling groups

There are three key proportions concerning siblings in various populations of children. First, well over 80 per cent of children in the population are members of sibling groups; secondly, approximately 30 to 40 per cent of children enter care with a sibling; thirdly, sibling groups referred to the 'special needs' agencies in our survey accounted for 25 per cent of all referrals to those agencies. This last figure is, of course, an under-estimate of the proportion of children who are referred for adoption since non-specialist agencies, i.e. those dealing with more 'normal' children, will tend to refer the sibling groups to the specialist agencies. There is a marked tendency for the referring agency to 'specify' that the group be maintained. Presumably where groups are to be split they will frequently be placed by the 'home' agency, and not referred.

What all of this indicates is that whatever the extent to which sibling groups are maintained intact by specialist agencies when placed in substitute families, very many sibling groups are split first by the process of reception into care, and subsequently by the process of referral for permanent placement.

Children placed

There can be little doubt that as far as sibling groups are concerned the specialist sector among placement agencies is very effective in securing the placement of children referred. Seven out of every eight children in sibling groups were placed or restored home to their family of origin. Moreover, among the 160 children in our sample there were only perhaps two who were clearly unlikely eventually to be placed or restored to the family of origin. Since many of these referred children were in the older age groups, and many of them had special needs in addition to being members of sibling groups, this represents a considerable achievement. Undoubtedly older children are among the more difficult ones to place, as our study confirms, but even in this respect local authorities wishing to locate placements for children and experiencing difficulty would be advised to try a range of possibilities and agencies since the system as a whole appears to be essentially very successful.

Maintaining or splitting the groups

Of the 141 children in our sample who were placed, only 17 were split from their siblings. On this evidence, seven children in every eight from referred sibling groups were placed with their brothers or sisters. The children who were split tended to have been longer on referral before placement. Where the placement seemed not to be working according to plan, there were moves in each direction, from splitting to restoring the sibling group, and from a maintained group into a split situation.

Perhaps given the overwhelming tendency for sibling groups to be maintained at placement, it is not surprising that this 'norm' is reflected in the records and thinking of adoption workers. Thus, there was a tendency not to record explicit reasons for maintaining groups of siblings where that was the course being pursued. On the other hand, much more detailed reasons were recorded where the intention was to split a group of siblings. By far the most frequent reason given for maintaining groups proved to be 'strong bond', an expression which recurred so frequently that it could be taken on the one hand for a 'catch-all' expression and on the other hand for an easy justification for the intended course of action.

Indeed, it is easy to be cynical about the use of the expression 'strong bond' and about the nature of sibling bonds themselves. If, as Timberlake and Hamlin (op. cit.) and Dunn (1988b) suggest, individual siblings modify their behaviour when with one another to take account each of the other's own circumstances, personality, etc., then what the adult observer witnesses might not reflect the actuality of the relationship. At an extreme, this must mean that adults cannot with any expectation of accuracy judge the strength of sibling relationships. Clearly, much fundamental research is needed on this topic before social worker assessments can be expected to represent accurately the strength of feeling between siblings and the importance of a possible splitting of the children concerned.

Our evidence was that the decision to split or to maintain was not related to reported positive or negative relationships between siblings; further, placement success, in the terms in which we were able to assess it, was not related to the presence of positive or negative feelings between siblings; moreover, placement success was not related to decisions to maintain or split sibling groups.

Superficially this evidence suggests two possibilities. First, an implication could be that the feelings towards one another of children in sibling groups can be safely ignored in reaching placement decisions since no significant differences were associated with placement outcome; a second view would be that given the lack of knowledge about the relative importance of sibling relationships in general and aspects of relationships in particular, then the assessment itself is bound to be crude and as yet inadequate to the task of discriminating appropriately between the children who would benefit most from a maintained and from a split group respectively; on this latter view, further knowledge should lead to better placement decisions.

Disruptions

The first point to make here is that disruptions are a very crude measure of success in placement. Nevertheless, they do represent a 'bottom line' and provide the indicator of success most frequently used both by researchers and by practitioners. The overall disruption rate of 21 per cent focusses on a negative aspect of the work. Naturally, agencies are concerned about situations which break down, represent failure, and bring trauma to those involved. On the other hand, it must not be forgotten that a disruption rate of 21 per cent implies a 'success' rate of 79 per cent of children in placements which had not broken down. This represents no mean achievement both by the professionals and the parents involved.

Among the issues which our research set out to address was whether the disruption rate among sibling groups was substantially higher than among singletons. Thoburn and Rowe (1988) provide a valuable comparison in their national survey of children in specialist voluntary agencies throughout Britain which reveals an average 21.5 per cent of children whose placement broke down. Although the periods of time during which children might have been exposed to placement breakdown varied between the national sample and our own regional exercise, the order of magnitude is comparable and suggests that the disruption rate among sibling groups is not appreciably different from that found amongst children overall. This is an important finding because a higher rate of disruption among sibling groups placed together might be expected; if the placement of one child in the sibling group broke down and as a consequence this was followed by a disruption for other children in that group, then overall such a higher rate of disruption among sibling groups would be explicable. This was the situation identified by Boyne et al. (1984), cited by Barth and Berry (1988). However, it was not found by Barth and Berry in their own research or in the present study which suggests that the sibling group introduces an additional liability in some situations, but offers additional strengths in others. Further suggestive evidence to support this is also provided by Thoburn and Rowe (op. cit.). The rate of disruption among our younger siblings was higher than that found in the national sample (19 per cent compared with 11 per cent) but the rate for older children was appreciably lower (26 per cent as against 37 per cent). As suggested above (Chapter 6), perhaps some younger children in sibling groups are more in jeopardy because of the problems of the older siblings if they are placed together; conversely, being placed with a younger sibling may reduce the chance of an older child being or feeling rejected by the new family.

The final consideration concerning disruptions is the lack of any statistically significant difference in the disruption rates of groups who were split and those who were maintained. As already mentioned, such a finding should not be taken to suggest that workers can be indiscriminate about maintaining or splitting groups and expect a similar outcome. On the contrary, it is to suggest that our present state of knowledge about sibling groups leaves problems spread relatively evenly. The task for the future is to focus on particular aspects, on characteristics of children and new families which will reduce even further the likelihood of placement breakdown.

Factors associated with disruption

Although disruption among the sibling groups was not higher than among other children (Thoburn and Rowe, op. cit.), the factors associated with disruption in our sample are different from those mentioned by Berridge and Cleaver (op. cit.) in their study of long-term fostering breakdowns. Thus, among children fostered, there were fewer breakdowns when the mothers were aged over forty, and when the parents had had previous experience. Evidence from our small study of sibling placements suggests that older mothers and those with previous parenting experience tended to be involved in more breakdowns. This difference between the two sets of findings could be explained by the different task being required of the groups of parents, but has been shown to reflect the composition of the substitute family itself.

Again, in the fostering study, there was a 50 per cent greater failure rate when children were completely separated from their siblings, compared with when they were placed together. In our study, this difference was reduced to the point where it failed to reach statistical significance.

Interestingly, in the fostering study, increased degrees of contact between children and their natural parents was related to a reduced level of breakdown, though this was not statistically significant. In our study, specifically among those who had spent a long time in care, links between children and their family of origin was also associated with a reduced risk of disruption.

The detailed analysis of disruptions has highlighted certain 'favoured' categories of children and has identified key factors, some of which help in understanding some differences found in the siblings study compared with other research.

In a number of respects the findings are not straightforward. For example, having additional 'special needs' (as well as belonging to a sibling group) was found not to be associated with rate of disruption when taken in conjunction with other relevant factors; when considered on its own, an association was found. Similarly, age of children at placement was not associated with disruptions among the sample as a whole, but proved an important factor for particular groups.

The first of the 'favoured categories' comprised children who were placed in families where they acquired new older step-siblings but where there was a gap of at least three years between the placed child and the step-sibling closest in age. Of the 17 such children, no placement broke down. By contrast, among the 27 children placed with new step-siblings where they were not the youngest, or not the youngest by at least three years, there were 14 disruptions, a rate of 52 per cent. Among children not placed in families with a new step-sibling the disruption rate was 16 per cent. This finding is similar in essence to those of Trasler (1960) and Parker (1966) in seminal studies of foster placements. It confirms the relevance of the composition of the substitute family to satisfactory outcome and the desirability of taking this fully into account in planning for placement.

As might be expected, a high proportion of these 'favoured' children were under 8 years of age (78 per cent), and younger children have been found in other studies to be less likely to disrupt (e.g. Thoburn and Rowe, op. cit.). Among the other group placed with new step-siblings, however, there was a high rate of disruption even where the children were young. Indeed the rate was higher among the ten children under eight (80 per cent) than among the 17 older children (35 per cent). This suggests that age of child is relevant, as well as the age-gap with the step-sibling nearest in age. The implications for placement decisions are clear - i.e. if placing children with new step-siblings it is better on average when placed children are younger by at least three years.

The second 'favoured' group of children were those who had spent a very short time in care prior to referral. Clearly, length of time in care could itself differentiate markedly between children from various circumstances but where links with the family were maintained at least to the referral stage, then the time in care was not associated with the rate of disruption. The maintenance of links with the child's family of origin is thus another important factor.

Further, time spent on referral also proved relevant to the rate of disruption - certainly among children placed without new step-siblings, or where there was a gap of less than three years between the placed child and the step-sibling nearest in age. Here, again, duration of time on referral before placement could in some situations reflect characteristics of the children rather than aspects of agency practice. It would seem important, however, that agencies and workers should examine practices in order to reduce wherever possible the time spent by children on referral, consistent with the child's needs and the appropriateness of a placement.

Finally, the detailed analysis confirmed the prima facie evidence that older mothers tended to be more commonly found where placements broke down. The picture is not straightforward, though. For children placed in families with new step-siblings, the mothers will by definition be likely to be older; as already discussed, the most important factor for them related to the age-gap with other siblings rather than the mother's age. Among children placed in childless new families, statistically significant evidence was found that the substitute mothers in placements which broke down tended on average to be older by several years than those where the placement did not break down. There was no evidence that older mothers found themselves with children who had additional 'special' needs. The findings suggest that for siblings placed in families which were hitherto childless, younger parents carry a lower risk of breakdown.

Without being unduly categorical, particularly given the scale of this research, there are obvious implications for practice from these pointers about the characteristics of the substitute family that imply varying degrees of risk of breakdown.

Links between family members

Research into the nature of sibling relationships suggests that although links between brothers and sisters are relatively little understood, they are nevertheless profound (Dunn, 1988a, b). Certainly, they are long-lasting, extend throughout much of life, and exceed in duration relationships with parents, children, or partners. It should surely, therefore, be the objective of all involved in placement activity to secure the best arrangements whereby children can have access to their siblings and maintain contact, even if tenuously. To date, 'access' has tended to be interpreted to mean access between child and parents, usually mother. But the relationship with siblings could prove to be more important, particularly where there is a rejecting or disturbed mother.

This will apply particularly to older children in need of placement, but even some of the younger children if split from their siblings could gain an increased sense of their own identity from a link with a 'lost' sibling. While with older children the benefits of links are more apparent, with younger children they could often be outweighed by the additional, and perhaps unacceptable complication involved for the substitute parents. To an extent this fine balancing by practitioners must be influenced by the perceived role of the substitute family; if they are seeking a child who, on an exclusive basis, will become a member of their family as if born to them then links must pose a threat; if, on the other hand, the substitute parents recognise a value in the shared care of the child and all parties can sustain the relationships appropriately, then links will be vitally important. Clearly, more knowledge is needed about the management of 'access' and 'links' in practice, building on the research evidence beginning to appear (Fratter, 1989).

Turning to links more generally, it is interesting to compare the attitudes enshrined both within the legal process and in the wider society to the separation of children from other members of their family through reception into care, adoption, and divorce. Where children are taken into care, elaborate legal provision exists to ensure that parents have some access; the position of grandparents in this respect is now strengthened. Where adoption is concerned, however, access arrangements are relatively rare. Indeed, adoption with access - or 'inclusive adoption' - is written about as a relatively new phenomenon, although it has existed on isolated occasion for very many years in Britain and is common in other cultures (Fratter, op. cit.). Now, though, it is being increasingly argued that there is a need to develop shared caring arrangements and to recognise that older children in care are likely to require long-term answers which are more appropriately found in fostering, residential or 'sheltered housing' situations but which in any event keep alive meaningful relationships with members of the family of orgin, e.g. Triseliotis (1986), Thoburn (1988), Wedge (1986b), Fallon et al. (1983), Millham et al. (1985). Such thinking underlies provision in the Children Act 1989.

As far as divorce is concerned, the main thrust of access arrangements, where children are being separated from one parent or other, has been to secure through legal judgement if necessary the accessibility of separated parent to child and vice versa. As the number of children placed with fathers increases, then there will be more groups of siblings split by the divorce process, and again access arrangements need to be considered by courts. The important difference about divorce proceedings, however, is that it is the business of the courts to secure appropriate access and to ensure that children can maintain their links with their family of origin, and can keep the identity that their birth parents have passed on to them. It is only reasonable to suppose that this will be an increasingly common concern in the field of adoption and other permanent substitute family arrangements as awareness increases and children's needs become more fully recognised - needs which include those of the sibling remaining with the birth family to have contact with the sibling in a long-term placement as well as vice versa (Mitchell, 1985; Maidment, 1984; Wallerstein and Kelly, 1980; Murch, 1980).

The current research provides some tentative evidence of the importance of links for the sibling groups studied. It was found that a longer time in care prior to referral was associated with increased placement breakdown among the groups included, but that this association disappeared where children had maintained links with their families of origin until referral. This study cannot indicate the 'mechanism' by which links operate and hence show a causal relationship. For the moment, though, it seems appropriate to use the evidence as indicative of the importance of links for a child who is away from the family of origin and awaiting placement, and for the relevant agency to strive to maintain contact with the family of origin accordingly. This is confirmed by evidence from post-adoption counselling agencies which have provided case examples illustrating the value of links with parents, siblings and other relatives (Howe and Hinings, 1989).

Implications for social work practice

As has been shown, the placement of the sibling groups studied has proved generally successful. Nevertheless, practice has been guided by 'hunch' and by theory transferred from other work with children rather than by research into the importance of sibling contact. As more knowledge becomes available then clearly this will need to be incorporated into the theory and practice of sibling placement. Meanwhile there are some lessons suggested by our study which draw on findings about (a) child and family characteristics associated with disruption, and (b) practice elements which appear to have contributed to placement breakdown.

Child and family characteristics

Some of the factors statistically associated with disruption (see Table 6.7 onwards), were found to overlap with one another in the more detailed analysis. For example, when other factors are also taken into account, the placements of children with 'special needs' in addition to their sibling status proved not to be more likely to break down than those without these needs or problems except among the older children in Group B; to some extent this will reflect the degree to which social work practitioners have succeeded in preparing substitute parents fully and in supporting the placement.

As far as care system factors are concerned, it is commonly understood that 'drift' in care should be avoided and that a decision about permanency should be made as early as possible in the child's care career. The findings reported here confirm that, and additionally show that long periods on referral to the specialist agency are also associated with increased risk of breakdown. The extent to which the children more likely to disrupt are those requiring longer on referral, or to which those experiencing a long period on referral are thereby more likely to disrupt is a dilemma which the current research cannot address. In any event, it seems important both to reduce to a minimum the length of time spent by children on referral consistent with finding an appropriate placement and to ensure that in the interim care is of good quality. The research also shows that where family links are maintained among children in care for long periods, then the length of time in care before referral ceases to be associated with disruption. The implication for social work practice is clear. Every effort should be made to ensure that children's links with their family of origin are maintained, not only because of parental rights and their involvement in the decision-making process, important as that is. The research suggests that family involvement also benefits the child even if permanent substitute placement is the course followed. Perhaps the enhancement of the sense of identity is crucial in this respect - but without more detailed investigation the specific mechanism can only be guessed. In its absence, it would seem obvious that involvement be encouraged and workers should even consider the possible desirability of re-establishing links where these have been lost.

As far as factors relating to the substitute family are concerned, there is likely to be considerable overlap. Older substitute mothers will be more likely to have had previous parenting experience and to be offering a home where there will more often be step-siblings. Put negatively, younger mothers will be less likely to have previous parenting experience and where they have none, then there will be no step-siblings for the study children. Although Berridge and Cleaver (op. cit.) reported different associated factors in their study of foster home breakdown, the circumstances for the groups of siblings in the current study are sufficiently different for them to be weighed in the balance when placement decisions are taken. It is possible that substitute parents can in general cope with sibling groups better where they have no specific preconceptions about children and siblings based on their own family; further, homes with no siblings might lead to better inter-child relations and less stress on parents than homes with existing siblings. On the other hand, where the age-gap is sufficient, placements of children with step-siblings and with older parents seem successful. The associations which have been identified do not necessarily imply causality or universality; they could, however, comprise indicators which require to be considered carefully by those engaged in family finding and which should be included in the factors to be taken into account.

Given the favoured groups identified in this study, there are clear pointers to some of the more desirable circumstances in the family of placement. First, where there are already children in the family it is advantageous when these are at least three years older than any newly placed child. This seems a particularly important factor.

Secondly, where there are no pre-existing children of the family, the placement is less likely to breakdown when the mother is younger rather than older.

Thus, children at highest risk of placement breakdown in our study were those who were younger than new step-siblings but by less than three years, or indeed were older than their new step-siblings; children were at high risk in such situations even if quite young in age (under 8 years) even though in other substitute family situations - and on average - these younger children would be least likely to experience placement breakdown (Thoburn and Rowe, op. cit.).

Finally, mention should be made of the length of time spent by children on referral. When a range of factors had been taken into account this remained significantly associated with placement disruption. It is therefore important for agencies and workers to review policies and practices, and attempt to reduce to a minimum the time spent by children on referral. Of course, the most difficult children to place could also be longest on referral and the more likely group to experience placement breakdown. They could be the most troubled children. In the absence of evidence to the contrary, however, it would seem best to act to reduce time on placement wherever possible in an attempt to reduce to a minimum the anxiety likely to be experienced by children, and in the process hope also to reduce disruption.

Practice elements

The next set of implications of the current study for social work practice concerns the reasons for placement breakdown of the sibling groups, as suggested by children's records (e.g. Table 6.3). Although the present 'placement system' is effective, perhaps it could be further improved. More attention could be given to helping the attachment of children and to supporting substitute parents in coping with behaviour difficulties, each of which was relevant in about 40 per cent of breakdowns; the possible conflict of loyalties between 'biological' and placed children (mentioned in 18 per cent of breakdowns) could be more thoroughly explored with substitute parents before and after placement is made and possibly much reduced if sufficient age-gap is ensured; mismanagement and poor practice by agency or worker, which occurred in a number of of disruptions, obviously need to be addressed and rectified.

These measures fall essentially within current frames of reference and practice knowledge. One reason for breakdown that fell outside, however, was the sustaining of links between separated siblings. It is interesting, too, that for some groups disruption was associated with the lack of links with any members of the child's family of origin. In view of the increasing evidence from psychological research of the relevance of sibling relationships, the maintenance of sibling links where children are separated assumes greater importance than hitherto realised or practised. Such links can meet needs both of children leaving their birth families and of those who remain behind (Thoburn, 1990).

The implications for social work practice of the need to maintain links are considerable, particularly as they involve a new set of relationships between substitute parents and children's families of origin. These are relationships which can be regarded as complicating an already fraught situation in securing sound placements. Daunting or not, it appears to be the direction in which innovation must move if the needs of children are to be satisfied and if children separated from brothers and sisters are to maintain an appropriate identity and be able to take it with them as they advance into adulthood. It seems desirable that where siblings are separated, even tenuous links might provide a means of children renewing closer contact should this be wanted in later years. To contrive such links without jeopardising the attachment to substitute parents is obviously a demanding and delicate matter which could prove impossible; in the present state of knowledge, however, it appears to be a worthy objective for which to aim.

It is, of course, also an objective relevant to many children in the care system who have become separated from their siblings either through the reception process or through placement. Despite the essential ignorance at present about the ways in which sibling relationships matter, the indications are that they are among each individual's most meaningful and longest-lasting relationships. The fact of their importance seems indisputable and social work practice must adapt accordingly.

Conclusion

In conclusion, the evidence from this study suggests that some of the lessons from foster care research published long ago (Trasler, 1980; Parker, 1966) have not been heeded; moreover, the selection of families for the placement of sibling groups could be improved. The importance of siblings to each other is a fact vital to all engaged in child care social work, particularly those involved in reception into care and placement in substitute families. Wherever practicable, in all social work activity with children and families, sibling relationships should be enabled to take their natural course in recognition of the (sometimes closet) importance of brothers and sisters to one another. When siblings must be separated then there remains a powerful case for ensuring that links between them are maintained so that in due course if they so wish the individuals can re-unite and re-locate themselves and their identity in that culture where their social understanding was begun.

References

Adcock, M. and White, R. (1985) 'Adoption, custodianship or fostering?', *Adoption and Fostering*, vol.9, no.4.
Aldgate, J. (1980) 'Identification of factors which influence length of stay in care' in Triseliotis, J. (q.v.).
Aldgate, J. and Hawley, D. (1986) 'Helping foster families through disruption', *Adoption and Fostering*, vol.10, no.2.
Aldridge, M. and Cautley, P. (1976) 'Placing siblings in the same foster home', *Child Welfare*, vol.55, no.2.
Argent, H. (1984) *Find me a family*, Souvenir Press, London.
Argent, H. (1988) *Keeping the doors open*, BAAF, London.
Bank, S.P. and Kahn, M.D. (1982a) *The Sibling Bond*, Basic Books, New York.
Bank, S.P. and Kahn, M.D. (1982b) 'Intense sibling loyalties' in Lamb, M.E. and Sutton-Smith, B. (eds.) (q.v.).
Barber, S. (1985) 'Planning access to children in care,' *Adoption and Fostering*, vol.9, no.3.
Barth, R.P. and Berry, M. (1987) 'Outcomes of child welfare services under permanency planning,' *Social Service Review*, University of Chicago, (March).
Barth, R.P. and Berry, M. (1988) *Adoption and disruption*, Aldine de Gruyter, New York.
Bellwood, P. (1985) 'Assessing siblings for family placement', *Adoption and Fostering*, vol.9, no.3.
Berridge, D. and Cleaver, H. (1987) *Foster home breakdown*, Blackwell, Oxford.
Boer, F. (1990) *Sibling relationships in middle childhood*, DSWO Press, Leiden.
Bowlby, J. (1951) *Maternal care and mental health*, World Health Organisation, Geneva.

Boyne, J., Denby, L., Kettenring, J.R. and Wheeler, W. (1984) *The shadow of success: a statistical analysis of outcomes of adoptions of hard-to-place children*, Spaulding for Children, Westfield, New Jersey.

Brenner, R.F. (1951) 'A follow-up study of adoptive families', cited in Pringle (1967).

Brody, G.H. and Stoneman, Z. (1982) 'Children with atypical siblings: socialisation outcomes and clinical participation' in Lehey, B. and Kazdin, A. (eds.) *Advances in Clinical Psychology*, vol.6, Plenum Press, New York.

Bryant, B.K. (1982) 'Sibling relationships in middle childhood' in Lamb, M.E. and Sutton-Smith. B. (eds.) (q.v.).

Cicirelli, V.G. (1976) 'Siblings teaching siblings' in Allen, V.L. (ed.) *Children as Teachers: theory and research on tutoring*, Academic Press, New York.

Clarke, A.M. and Clarke, A.D.B. (1976) *Early experience: myth and evidence*, Open Books, London.

Clifton, J. (1985) 'A preliminary investigation of the sibling dimension for children in care'. (Unpublished dissertation. Goldsmiths College, University of London).

Cousins, J. (1989) 'Keeping siblings together', *Social Work Today*, vol.20, no.30.

Cowley, L. (1987) Letter re 'splitting siblings' in *Adoption and Fostering*, vol.11, no.2.

Cutler, J.P. (1984) 'A study of children in foster care: problems related to the separation of siblings'. Dissertation submitted to the Catholic University of America and cited in *Dissertation Abstracts International*, vol.45.

Dale, N. (1989) 'Pretend play with mothers and siblings: relations between early performance and partners', *Journal of Child Psychology and Psychiatry*, vol.30, no.5

DHSS (1983) *Code of Practice on Access to Children in Care*, HMSO, London.

DHSS (1984) *Children in care in England and Wales, March 1984*, HMSO, London.

Donley, K. (1978) 'The dynamics of disruption', *Adoption and Fostering*, vol.2, no.2.

Dresser, I. (1985) 'Psychological homelessless, a clinical example', *Journal of Social Work Practice*, vol.1, no.4.

Dunn, J. (1984) *Sisters and Brothers*, Fontana, London.

Dunn, J. (1988a) 'Sibling influences on childhood development', *Journal of Child Psychology and Psychiatry*, vol.29, no.2.

Dunn, J. (1988b) *The beginnings of social understanding*, Blackwell, Oxford.

Dunn, J. and Kendrick, C. (1982) *Siblings*, Grant McIntyre, London.

Eekelaar, J. and Clive, E.M. (1977) *Custody after divorce*, Centre for Socio-Legal Studies, Oxford.

Fahlberg, V. (1981) *Attachment and Separation*, BAAF Practice Series, no.5, London.

Fallon, M., McKenna, M., Waring, P., Wilson, G., Thom, M. and Giltinan, D. (1983) 'Placing adolescents in families', *Adoption and Fostering*, vol.7, no.4.

Fanshel, D. and Shinn, E.B. (1978) *Children in foster care: a longitudinal investigation*, Columbia University Press, New York.

Festinger, T. (1986) *Necessary risk: a study of adoptions and disrupted adoptive placements*, Child Welfare League of America, New York.

Fitzgerald, J. (1983) *Understanding disruption*, BAAF, London.

Forbes, L.M. (1977) 'Obstacles to placement', *Adoption and Fostering*, vol.1, no.4.

Fratter, J. (1989) *Family placement and access: achieving permanency for children in contact with birth parents*, Barnardos, Ilford.

Fratter, J., Rowe, J., Sapsford, D. and Thoburn, J. (forthcoming) *Outcomes of permanent family placement*, BAAF, London.

Goldstein, J., Freud, A. and Solnit, A.J. (1973) *Beyond the best interests of the child*, Free Press, New York.

Goldstein, J., Freud, A. and Solnit, A.J. (1980) *Before the best interests of the child*, Burnett/Deutsch, London.

Greenbaum, M. (1965) 'Joint sibling interview as a diagnostic procedure', *Journal of Child Psychology and Psychiatry*, vol.6.

Hapgood, M. (1984) 'Older child adoption and knowledge base of adoption practice' in Bean, P. (ed.) *Adoption*, Tavistock, London.

Haskey, J. (1982) 'The proportion of marriages ending in divorce', *Population Trends*, no.27, HMSO, London.

Haskey, J. (1983) 'Children of divorcing couples', *Population Trends*, no.31, HMSO, London.

Hodges, J. and Tizard, B. (1989) 'Social and family relationships of ex-institutional adolescents', *Journal of Child Psychology and Psychiatry*, vol.30, no.1.

Holman, R. (1980) 'Exclusive and inclusive concepts of fostering' in Triseliotis, J. (ed.) (q.v.).

Howe, D. (1988) 'Survey of initial referrals to the Post-Adoption Centre', *Adoption and Fostering*, vol.12, no.1.

Howe, D. and Hinings, D. (1989) 'The Post-Adoption Centre: the first three years', *Research Report no. 3 (Adopted People)*, University of East Anglia, Norwich.

Jacka, A. (1973) *Adoption in brief*, National Foundation for Educational Research, Windsor.

Johnson, D. (1986) 'Access: the natural family's dilemma', *Adoption and Fostering*, vol.10, no.3.

Jones, M. and Niblett, R. (1985) 'To split or not to split: the placement of siblings', *Adoption and Fostering*, vol.9, no.2.

Kadushin, A. (1970) *Adopting older children*, Columbia University Press, New York.

Koch, H.L. (1960) *The relation of certain formal attributes of siblings to attitudes held toward each other and toward their parents*. Monographs of the Society for Research in Child Development, no.25.

Lahti, J. (1982) 'A follow-up study of foster children in permanent placements', *Social Services Review*, University of Chicago.

Lamb, M.E. (1982a) in Lamb, M.E. and Sutton-Smith, B. (eds.) (q.v.).
Lamb, M.E. (1982b) 'Paternal Influences on Early Socio-Emotional Development', *Journal of Child Psychology and Psychiatry*, vol.12, no.2.
Lamb, M.E. and Sutton-Smith, B. (eds.) (1982) *Sibling relationships: their nature and significance across the lifespan*, Lawrence Erlbaum Associates, Hillsdale, New Jersey.
Lambert, L. and Streather, J. (1980) *Children in changing families*, Macmillan, London.
Lavigueur, H. (1976) 'The use of siblings as an adjunct to the behavioural treatment of children in the home with parents as therapists', *Behaviour Therapy*, vol.7.
Levy, D.M. (1934) 'Rivalry between children of the same family', *Child Study*, vol.11.
Levy, D.M. (1937) *Studies in sibling rivalry*, American Orthopsychiatry Research Monograph, no.2.
Lewis, T. and Wedge, P. (in preparation) 'Group and individual factors in the outcome of sibling placement'.
Macaskill, C. (1986) 'Post adoption support' in Wedge, P. and Thoburn, J. (eds.) (q.v.).
Madge, N. (1983) *Families at Risk*, Heinemann, London.
Maidment, S. (1976) 'A study in child custody', *Family Law*, vol.6, Nos. 7 and 8.
Maidment, S. (1984) *Child Custody and Divorce*, Croom Helm, London.
Maier, H.W. (1981) 'Essential components in care and treatment environments for children' in Ainsworth, F. and Fulcher, L.C. (eds.) *Group care for children: concept and issues*, Tavistock, London.
Mednick, S.A., Gabrielli, W.F. and Hutchings, B. (1984) 'Genetic influences in criminal convictions: evidence from an adoption cohort', *Science*, vol.22, no.4.
Meyer, D.J., Vadasy, P.R. and Fewell, R.R. (1986) *Living with a brother or sister with special needs*, University of Washington Press, Washington.
Millham, S., Bullock, R., Hosie, K. and Haak, M. (1986) *Lost in Care*. Gower, Aldershot.
Millham, S., Bullock, R., Hosie, K. and Little, M. (1985) 'Maintaining family links of children in care', *Adoption and Fostering*, vol.9, no.2.
Mitchell, A. (1985) *Children in the middle: living through divorce*, Tavistock, London.
Morris, C. (1984) *The permanency principle in child care social work*, Social Work Monographs, University of East Anglia, Norwich.
Morrison, T. and Brown, J. (1986) 'Splitting siblings', *Adoption and Fostering*, vol.10, no.4.
Murch, M. (1980) *Justice and welfare in divorce*, Sweet and Maxwell, London.
Nix, H. (1983) Sibling relationships in older child adoptions', *Adoption and Fostering*, vol.7, no.2.
OPCS (1986) *Marriage and divorce statistics 1984*, Office of Population Census and Surveys Monitor, FM2, 11.

Packman, J., Randall, J. and Jacques, N. (1986) *Who needs care? Social work decisions about children in care and their families*, Blackwell, Oxford.
Page, R. and Clark, G.A. (eds.) (1977) *Who cares? Young people in care speak out*. National Children's Bureau, London.
Parke, R.D. (1981) *Fathering*. Fontana, London.
Parker, R. (1966) *Decisions in childcare*, Allen and Unwin, London.
Pringle, M..K. (1967) *Adoption facts and fallacies*, Longmans, London.
Pringle, M.K. (1974) *The Needs of Children*, Hutchinson, London.
Proch, K. and Howard, J.A. (1986) 'Parental visiting of children in foster care', *Social Work*, vol.31, no.3.
Reich, D. and Lewis, J. (1986) 'Placements by Parents for Children' in Wedge, P. and Thoburn, J. (eds.) (q.v.).
Rimmer, L. (1981) *Families in focus*. Study Commission on the Family, London.
Ross, H.G. and Milgram, J.I. (1982) 'Important variables in adult sibling relationships: a qualitative study' in Lamb, M.E. and Sutton-Smith, B. (eds.) (q.v.).
Rowe, J. (1987) 'Fostering outcomes: interpreting breakdown rates', *Adoption and Fostering*, vol.11, no.1.
Rowe, J., Cain, H., Hundleby, M. and Keane, A. (1984) *Long-term foster care*. Batsford, London.
Rushton, A., Treseder, J. and Quinton, D. (1989) 'Sibling groups in permanent placements', *Adoption and Fostering*, vol.13, no.4.
Rutter, M. (1981) *Maternal deprivation re-assessed*, Penguin Books, Harmondsworth.
Sawbridge, P. (1983) *Parents for Children*, BAAF, London.
Sawbridge, P. (1988) 'The Post-Adoption Centre - what are the users teaching us?', *Adoption and Fostering*, vol.12, no.1.
Seale, S. (1984) *Children in divorce: a study of information available to the Scottish Courts on children involved in divorce actions*, Scottish Office Central Research Unit.
Seglow, J., Pringle, M.K. and Wedge, P. (1972) *Growing up adopted*, National Foundation for Educational Research, Windsor.
Skeels, H.M. and Harms, I. (1948) 'Children with inferior social histories: their mental development in adoptive homes' cited in Pringle (1967) (q.v.).
Stewart, R.B. (1984) 'Sibling interaction: the role of the older child as teacher for the younger', *Merrill-Palmer Quarterly*, vol. 29, no.1.
Sutton-Smith, B. (1966) 'Role replication and reversal in play', *Merrill-Palmer Quarterly*, no.12.
Sutton-Smith, B. and Rosenberg, B.G. (1970) *The Sibling*, Holt, Rinehart and Wilson, New York.
Thoburn, J. (1988) *Child placement: Principles and Practice*, Gower/Wildwood, Aldershot.
Thoburn, J. (1990) *Success and failure in permanent family placement*, Avebury/Gower, Aldershot.
Thoburn, J., Murdoch, A. and O'Brien, A. (1986) *Permanence in Child Care*, Blackwell, Oxford.

Thoburn, J. and Rowe, J. (1988) 'A snapshot of permanent family placement', Adoption and Fostering, vol.12, no.3.
Timberlake, E.M. and Hamlin, E.R. (1982) 'The sibling group: a neglected dimension of placement', Child Welfare, vol.61, no.8.
Tizard, B. (1977) Adoption: a second chance, Open Books, London.
Trasler, G. (1960) In place of parents, Routledge and Kegan Paul, London.
Triseliotis, J. (1980) New developments in foster care and adoption, Routledge and Kegan Paul, London.
Triseliotis, J. (1985) 'Adoption with contact', Adoption and Fostering, vol.9, no.4.
Triseliotis, J. (1986) 'Older children in care' in Wedge, P. and Thoburn, J. (eds) (q.v.).
Triseliotis, J. and Russell, J. (1984) Hard to place, Heinemann, London.
Wallerstein, J.S. and Kelly, J.B. (1980) Surviving the breakup: how children and parents cope with divorce, Grant McIntyre, New York.
Ward, M. (1984) 'Sibling ties in foster care and adoption placing', Child Welfare, no.63.
Ward, S. (1986) 'Open adoption: two case examples', Adoption and Fostering, vol.10, no.2.
Wedge, P. (1986a) 'Family finding in Essex' in Wedge, P. and Thoburn, J. (eds.) (q.v.).
Wedge, P. (1986b) 'Lessons from research into permanent family placement' in Wedge, P. and Thoburn, J. (eds.) (q.v.).
Wedge, P. and Phelan, J. (1986) Essex Child Care Survey 1981-85, Social Work Development Unit, University of East Anglia, Norwich.
Wedge, P. and Thoburn, J. (eds.) (1986) Finding families for hard-to-place children, BAAF, London.
Weisner, T.S. (1982) 'Sibling interdependence and child caretaking: a cross cultural view' in Lamb, M.E. and Sutton-Smith, B. (eds.) (q.v.).
Wilson, B. and Edington, G. (1982) First child, second child: what your birth order means to you. Souvenir Press, London.
Wolkind, S. and Kozaruk, A. (1986) 'Hard-to-place? Children with medical and developmental problems' in Wedge, P. and Thoburn, J. (eds.) (q.v.).
Youniss, J. (1980) Parents and peers in social development. University of Chicago Press, Chicago and London.

Appendix: information gathered for the study

1. Time study-child had spent in care at referral/acceptance point.
2. Links with family of origin at referral/acceptance point.
3. Links with family of origin at the six months point after placement began.
4. Sex of study child.
5. Age of study child at referral/acceptance point.
6. The homefinding agency accepting the study child on referral.
7. Whether the study child has at least one special need (additional to membership of a sibling group).
8. Number of special needs (additional to membership of a sibling group)?
9. Additional special needs.
10. Whether the study child was permanently placed.
11. Time study child spent on referral before being permanently placed.

12. Whether the permanent substitute placement broke down (i.e. excluding those children restored to their families).

13. The first documented aim for the study child's group.

14. Whether sibling group maintained, etc. in the first permanent placement.

15. The number of siblings of the study child.

16. Whether the study child was restored to its family of origin.

17. The amount documented about the study child's patterns of interaction with his/her siblings, before placement.

18. Whether option(s) to the first aim were documented.

19. Assessment of the permanent substitute placement six months after it began (or as near as possible to six months).

20. Latest assessment of the permanent substitute placement available (6 months-3 years).

21. Time from beginning of permanent substitute placement to latest assessment, in days.

22. Age of substitute mother when placement began.

23. Previous parenting experience of the new parents.

24. The number of new step-siblings for the study child.

25. The age of the study child in relation to his/her new step-sibling(s).

26. The age difference between the study child and his/her new step-sibling closest in age.

27. Study child's age in relation to new step-siblings and natural/step-siblings from family of origin placed with him/her.

28. Criteria used by social workers in their assessment of the permanent substitute placements.

29. Length of permanent substitute placement in days in cases where the placement had broken down.

30. Whether the study child was adopted.

31. Links with the family of origin at the referral/acceptance point.

32. Links with the family of origin at the six months point after the permanent substitute placement began.

33. The study child's patterns of interaction with other sibling group members.

34. Parents, children and professionals whose viewpoints were considered in reaching first aim.

35. Whether there was a reason explicit for the selected aim.

36. The main reason given for the selection of the aim.

37. The destination of those children who suffered break down of their permanent substitute placement.

Index of authors

Adcock (and White), 16
Aldgate, 15
Aldgate (and Hawley), 13, 15, 24, 55, 56
Aldridge (and Cautley), 4
Argent (1984), 23
(1988), 24

Bank (and Kahn) (1982a), 10
(1982b), 10
Barber, 15
Barth (and Berry) (1987), 45
Barth (and Berry) (1988), 46
Bellwood, 13
Berridge (and Cleaver), 4, 16, 46, 58, 59, 60, 63, 76, 81
Berry (Barth and Berry) (1987), 45
Berry (Barth and Berry) (1988), 76
Boer, 10
Bowlby, 2
Boyne (et al), 76
Brenner, 21
Brody (and Stoneman), 10
Brown (Morrison and Brown), 4
Bryant, 10

Cautley (Aldridge and Cautley), 4
Cicirelli, 10
Clark (Page and Clark), 15
Clarke (and Clarke), 9, 13
Cleaver (Berridge and Cleaver), 4, 16, 46, 58, 59, 60, 63, 76, 81
Clifton, 5
Clive (Eekelaar and Clive), 18
Cousins, 5
Cowley, 4
Cutler, 4

Dale, 10
DHSS (1983), 14
(1984), 31
Donley, 15, 55, 56
Dresser, 4
Dunn (1984), 8, 9
(1988a), 11, 13, 78
(1988b), 11, 75, 78
Dunn (and Kendrick), 2

Edington (Wilson and Edington), 9
Eekelaar (Eekelaar and Clive), 18

Fahlberg, 13

Fallon (et al.), 79
Fanshel (and Shinn), 4, 15
Festinger, 24
Fitzgerald, 55
Forbes, 4, 36
Fratter, 14, 16, 22, 79
Fratter (et al.), 16

Goldstein (et al.) (1973), 15
Goldstein (et al.) (1980), 14
Greenbaum, 10

Hamlin (Timberlake and Hamlin), 5, 36, 75
Hapgood, 20
Harms (Skeels and Harms), 20
Haskey (1982), 17
         (1983), 17
Hawley (Aldgate and Hawley), 13, 15, 24, 55, 56
Hinings (Howe and Hinings), 80
Hodges (and Tizard), 24
Holman, 15
Howard (Proch and Howard), 15
Howe, 17
Howe (and Hinings), 80

Jacka, 20
Johnson, 15
Jones (and Niblett), 2, 5, 12

Kadushin, 24
Kahn (Bank and Kahn), 10
Kelly (Wallerstein and Kelly), 18, 19, 80
Koch, 10
Kozaruk (Wolkind and Kozaruk), 21, 22

Lahti, 24
Lamb (1982a), 8, 9
     (1982b), 2
Lamb (and Sutton-Smith), 2
Lambert (and Streather), 24
Lavigueur, 10
Levy (1934), 10
     (1937), 10
Lewis (Reich and Lewis), 22, 23
Lewis (and Wedge), 72

Macaskill, 24, 27
Madge, 2
Maidment (1976), 18
         (1984), 18, 80
Maier, 15
Mednick, 22
Meyer (et al.), 10
Milgram (Ross and Milgram), 8
Millham (et al.) (1985), 79
                 (1986), 4, 12, 14, 15, 16, 30
Mitchell, 17, 18, 19, 80
Morris, 15
Morrison (and Brown), 4
Murch, 18, 80

Niblett (Jones and Niblett), 2, 5, 12
Nix, 4

OPCS, 17

Packman (et al.), 12, 15
Page (and Clark), 15
Parke, 2
Parker, 47, 77, 83
Phelan (Wedge and Phelan), 12, 30, 31
Pringle (1967), 20, 21, 22
        (1974), 2
Proch (and Howard), 15

Reich (and Lewis), 22
Rimmer, 17
Rosenberg (Sutton-Smith and Rosenberg), 10
Ross (and Milgram), 8
Rowe, 8, 25, 50.
Rowe (et al.), 2, 4, 12, 15, 16, 20, 23, 24, 30
Rowe (Thoburn and Rowe), 4, 22, 27, 43, 50, 51, 55, 60, 63, 76, 77, 82
Rushton (et al.), 7
Russell (Triseliotis and Russell), 24
Rutter, 2

Sawbridge (1983), 23
          (1988), 17
Seale, 18
Seglow (et al.), 24
Shinn (Fanshel and Shinn), 15
Skeels (and Harms), 20
Stewart, 10

Stoneman (Brody and Stoneman), 10
Streather (Lambert and Streather), 24
Sutton-Smith, 10, 13
Sutton-Smith (Bank and Sutton-Smith), 2
Sutton-Smith (and Rosenberg), 10

Thoburn (1988), 79
      (1990), 24, 49, 83
Thoburn (et al)., 16, 20, 21, 23, 24
Thoburn (and Rowe), 4, 22, 27, 43, 50, 51, 55, 60, 63, 76, 77, 82
Thoburn (Wedge and Thoburn), 2, 20
Timberlake (and Hamlin), 5, 36, 75
Tizard, 22
Tizard (Hodges and Tizard), 24
Trasler, 47, 77, 83
Triseliotis (1980), 24
          (1985), 13
          (1986), 17, 22, 45, 79
Triseliotis (and Russell), 24

Wallerstein (and Kelly), 18, 19, 80
Ward (M), 4
Ward (S), 13, 16
Wedge (1986a), 23
    (1986b), 23, 45, 79
Wedge (and Phelan), 12, 30, 31
Wedge (and Thoburn), 2, 20
Wedge (Lewis and Wedge), 72
Weisner, 9
White (Adcock and White), 16
Wilson (and Edington), 9
Wolkind (and Kozaruk), 21, 22

Youniss, 8

DATE DUE

MAY 04 1999			
FEB 2 6 2002			
GAYLORD			PRINTED IN U.S.A.